CABARET McGONAGALL

Books by W.N. Herbert

POETRY

Sterts & Stobies, with Robert Crawford (Obog Books, 1985)
Sharawaggi, with Robert Crawford (Polygon, 1990)
The Landfish (Duncan of Jordanstone College of Art, 1991)
Dundee Doldrums (Galliard, 1991)
Anither Music (Vennel Press, 1991)
The Testament of the Reverend Thomas Dick (Arc Publications, 1994)
Forked Tongue (Bloodaxe Books, 1994)
Cabaret McGonagall (Bloodaxe Books, 1996)

LITERARY CRITICISM

To Circumjack MacDiarmid (Oxford University Press, 1992)

CABARET McGonagall

W.N. HERBERT

BLOODAXE BOOKS

ISBN: 1 85224 353 8

First published 1996 by
Bloodaxe Books Ltd,
P.O. Box 1SN,
Newcastle upon Tyne NE99 1SN.

Bloodaxe Books Ltd acknowledges
the financial assistance of Northern Arts.

Cover printing by J. Thomson Colour Printers Ltd, Glasgow.

Printed in Great Britain by
Cromwell Press Ltd, Broughton Gifford, Melksham, Wiltshire.

'He was an old man, but, with his athletic though slightly stooping figure and his dark hair, he did not look more than forty-five: and he appeared to have been shaved the night before. He wore a Highland dress of Rob Roy tartan and boy's size. After reciting some of his own poems, to an accompaniment of whistles and cat-calls, the Bard armed himself with a most dangerous-looking broadsword, and strode up and down the platform, declaiming 'Clarence's dream' and 'Give me another horse – bind up my wounds.' His voice rose to a howl. He thrust and slashed at imaginary foes. A shower of apples and oranges fell on the platform. Almost before they touched it, they were met at the fell edge of McGonagall's claymore and cut to pieces. The Bard was beaded with perspiration and orange juice. The audience yelled with delight; Mc-Gonagall yelled louder still, with a fury which I fancy was not wholly feigned. It was like a squalid travesty of the wildest scenes of *Don Quixote* and *Orlando Furioso*. I left the hall early, saddened and disgusted.'

WILLIAM POWER

'Dada is working with all its might towards the universal installation of the idiot.'

TRISTAN TZARA

ACKNOWLEDGEMENTS

Acknowledgements are due to the editors of the following publications in which some of these poems first appeared: *Angel Exhaust, Aynd, Broken Fiddle, The Cartoonist, Chapman, Edinburgh Review, Ibid, Iron, Lines Review, London Magazine, Markings, New Writing Scotland, Pigeonhole, PN Review, Poetry Review, The Printer's Devil, Red Herring, The Scotsman, Verse* and *The Wide Skirt.*

Several poems have been broadcast by BBC Radio 3, who also commissioned 'Song of the Terrible Lizard'.

Several poems also appeared in the anthology *Contraflow on the Superhighway* (Southfields, 1994).

'Road Movie' was commissioned by the Poetry Library, Morpeth, as part of its exhibition *Moving On: A Celebration of Road Movies.*

I would like to express my gratitude to Dumfries and Galloway Arts Association, Moray District Council, and the Universities of Newcastle and Durham, as well as to the Scottish Arts Council and Northern Arts, for the residencies and fellowship which supported me during the writing of this book. In particular, I'd like to thank Jenny Wilson, Graham McDermid and Jenny Attala.

CONTENTS

Low Road

Congratulations. You're entering a zone
where all signs are bilingual in deference,
but not to your tongue. Where all the references,
though scholarly, are to an unknown
culture. Everyone else here knows the road:
they stride through the anomalies
like cool arcades; swim in homilies
deep as glog-holes like eyeless toads.
      It's only you
still hoping that you'll just pass through.

For here Joyburgh's twinned with Panicville,
but built so near you constantly recheck
your pocket guidebook's screen, which likes
renaming the streets; the borders swill
like lines of ants. Its cover used to show
the statue of some unpronounceable,
now it's the new parliament – possibly –
and 'used to' means the day before – or used to.
      You used to be sure
that you were passing through.

But when you go somewhere by car it takes
seven years – anywhere, no matter how
close or far, though it's never far enough
for someone who's attempting to escape.
At least you never age according
to the mirrors. All the packaging suffers
from Tourette's syndrome: SKUM is marsh-
mallows, milk products GUK, and lard is HARDON.
      You tell yourself 'So?
What I eat's just passing through.'

You meet the absences of others –
'Where are the words that would have come, that did
for years of stilling into staleness...' – hidden
in old scribbles on the cafés' papers,
like postcards that nobody has sent you:

'Congratulations. This product is past
its sell-by date. This makes its value last
and it safe to consume (not that you intend to).'
        These must by now
(you hope) have passed on through.

By now a woman's marked you, always there
before you in whichever city;
perhaps she forged all this graffiti.
You blunder past her but she mutters:
'We're waiting for the one thing science said
it can explain to us precisely: how
we'll die. We bring ourselves the pharaohs'
mountains, brick by brick, and heap them on our heads.
        Nice view,
unless you're under it, and think you're passing through.'

GONE WEST

'From the bonny bells of heather
They brewed a drink langsyne,
Was sweeter far than honey,
Was stronger far than wine.
They brewed it and they drank it.
And lay in a blessed swound
For days and days together
In their dwellings underground.'

ROBERT LOUIS STEVENSON

'I've always had access to other worlds. We all do because
we all dream. What I don't have access to is myself.'

LEONORA CARRINGTON

The King and Queen of Dumfriesshire

The King and Queen of Dumfriesshire sit
in their battery-dead Triumph, gazing ahead
at an iced-over windscreen like a gull rolled flat.
They are cast in bronze, with Henry Moore holes
shot in each other by incessant argument;
these are convenient for holding her tartan flask,
his rolled-up *Scotsman*. The hairy skeleton
of a Border terrier sits in the back window,
not nodding. On the back seat rests
their favourite argument, the one about
how he does not permit her to see the old friends
she no longer likes and he secretly misses;
the one which is really about punishing each other
for no longer wanting to make love.
The argument is in the form of a big white bowl
with a black band around it hand-painted with fruit.
It has a gold rim, and in it lies
a brown curl of water from the leaking roof.
Outside, the clouds continue
to bomb the glen with sheep, which bare
their slate teeth as they tumble,
unexpectedly sneering.
The King and Queen of Dumfriesshire sit
like the too-solid bullet-ridden ghosts
of Bonny and Clyde, not eating their
tinned salmon sandwiches, crustless, still
wrapped in tinfoil, still in the tupperware.
They survey their domain, not glancing at
each other, not removing from the glove compartment
any of the old words they have always used,
words like 'twae', like 'couthy', like 'Kirkcudbright',
which keep their only threat at bay: of separation.

Ballad of the House of Fear
(variation on a theme by Leonora Carrington)

Eh've bideit in thi Hoose o Fear
as fowk bide in a howf,
Eh've sippit fear fur fehv lang year
an thi bree is daurk an dowf.

Thi Deil's in thi Hoose o Fear
tho nivir therr tae meet:
he shaves his horns intil yir beer,
his sharn's in whit yi eat.

Eh dwallit in thi Hoose o Fear
an medd a bed o dreid,
an mony baists werr gaithert there
that yestirdey hud dee'd.

An here's thi moose that baudrins paad
whas neck Eh hud tae brak,
an here's thi doe whas fleesh Eh chaad,
ma teeth-mairks innur back.

An wingless baukie-burds gae pat-
a-pingle in thi rug,
and aa thi tears yi ivir grat
ur gaithirt i thi jug.

Sae here's a cup tae thi cuddie's health
De Chirico did see,
that Leonora kent in wealth
an psychic miserie.

Gee me yir hoof, ma gallant Horse,
yir gallop's hoo Eh think,
an lyk a quick man wi a corse,
thigithir we sall drink.

Thi sel is like a brittul gless,
twa spirals innuts stem,
thi sel wull crack at Fear's request
gin that's jist an 'ahem'.

bree: brew; *dowf*: deep; *sharn*: excrement; *baudrins*: the cat; *paad*: pawed; *baukie-burds*: bats; *pingil*: to struggle; *grat*: wept; *cuddie*: horse; *corse*: corpse;

Thi sel is like thi random foarm
in whilk a hare ligs doon;
thi gress is flaird by ilka stoarm
that wallochs owre thi groon.

There's mony fowk whas cup is split
and aa's slaw-seepit oot,
till naethin's left but a dreggy glit
o aa they werr aboot.

There's unca foarms that clean explode
at Fear's castrato voice,
as bluidy assa puffed-up toad
yet still yi maun rejoice.

Fur i thi Hoose o Fear there's wan
sma detail aften missed;
there's nane sae free frae thi Deil's plan
as thae wha Fear huz kissed.

Tae gee anithir grief's thi same
as awnin til thi fact
Grief's mithir's stappit in yir wame
and, when she wull, comes back.

Eh dwallit in thi Hoose o Fear
assa hare bides in a hollow;
Eh cudnae laive thon hoose fur fear
that Fear utsel wad follow.

Thi lichts werr bleezin dey an nicht,
thi clash wiz lood an fast;
there's nocht that gees yi sic a fricht
as thi thocht that fear is past.

But unca fowk can tak thir cheer
tho thi door is aff thi snib:
Eh've bideit in thi Hoose o Fear
an wi them aa ur sib.

---

wallochs: ranges freely; *glit*: greasy, sticky matter; *unca*: a few, unusual; *stappit*:
rammed down; *sib*: related.

The Pheasant Lesson

Every evening, the Metro stumbling
home from school, I'd disturb
at the same point up
the two mile track to my cottage
the same two deer. They'd leap
my headlights, landing in
the usual storm of darkness
that swept up from Portpatrick
to Dunskey, carrying off my electricity,
my phonecalls, the storm-door from
its hinges, and crashing all these
through the harmonica trees
like pheasants' wings.

Every morning, the Metro grunting
schoolwards, I'd dodge
potholes and pheasants in
equal droves, always in their places
like dull brown starmaps.
The hens cleared off pronto, but
the cocks found it hard to decide
between losing face
and becoming game paste,
and strutted slowly from beneath my wheels.

One day the lane was full
of clean Landrovers, waxy Barbours,
and gun-bright faces staring at
my broke-bumpered, crud-sullied, door-dented,
formerly-white Metro.
I wound the window down
and grinned 'Good morning!'
to a chorus of blanks:
the women's eyes ran for the bushes
and the men's double-barrelled gaze
bore through the burr in my voice.
I thought: get out of their sights.

That night the deer didn't show,
didn't jump, and the woods had been shaved
of a churring noise I only noticed now
it was gone. My mind drove back
to a long thin room
in the Carse of Gowrie, lined
with hooks at shoulder height,
like corridors outside old classrooms.
After a shoot it would be hung
with bleary braces, pheasants slung
like children's raincoats.

And from a T-bar at the end,
hooked through its shanks,
hanging with its head in
a bloody bucket,
would be a deer. It looked
as though it had been caught
in mid-leap, before
it could make the darkness, be
washed through the trees
away where all my phonecalls had
collected, where my lesson for
tomorrow would be forming.

The Anxiety of Information

What is the tribe among whom women conceive
at the age of five
and die at the age of eight?
What is the tribe whose smell
puts crocodiles to flight?
Is it true that the ibis can be regarded as
the inventor of the enema?
Which is the bird that goes bald
in the turnip season?
What connection exists between
the lobes of the liver of the mouse
and the phases of the moon?

What is the name of the King of Epirus whose
big toe cured diseases
of the spleen?
The name of the woman of ancient Rome
who never spat?
The name of the historian who paid 21,000f
for a plate of speaking birds' tongues?
Of the poet whose mistress received
the attentions of an elephant?

Is it true that female quails
are so lascivious
that it is enough for them to hear the voice
of the male
in order to conceive?
That a serpent barked
when the Tarquins were expelled?
That Aristomenes of Messena,
who killed 300 Spartans,
had a heart made of hair?

Featherhood
(for Debbie)

1

God speaks in sic undeemis weys
that maist o whit he seys
gaes maunderin awa
in pirrs an pirlies lyk
a speugie soomin thru a hedge,

or thi soond o an ice-cream van
prinklin uts notes thru a gloamin estate
in Stranraer,
in thi middle o Januar:

ut seems ut maun be meagrims till
He talks ti you in pain
an the meisslin awa o pain,
in solace and
uts meisslin awa.

2

This is thi wey Eh didnae ken
why thi flaffin flicht
o three grey wullie-wagtails
straicht
in frunt o ma car
filld me wi mair nor fricht

until
parkd in Castle Douglas
Eh thocht o the computer's
photie o wir ain three eggs
abstractit fae yir boady
an fertilised
by IVF:

undeemis: extraordinary; *maundering*: sounding indistinctly; *pirrs an pirlies*: gentle
breaths and small things; *speugie*: sparrow; *soomin*: swimming; *prinklin*: bubbling;
meagrims: absurd notions; *meisslin*: wasting imperceptibly; *flaffin*: a fluttering of
the wings.

18

that tho yirdit in
yir willin wame
came loose
an flew awa.

3

An kennan this repleyed
thae ithir flee's-wing instants,
nearly stills:

o starin thru a screen intil
thi ocean o yir kelder
lyk a submariner
lukean fur the sonar ding
o wir twa-munth dochtir's
foetal hert;

o sittan in
thi doctir's oaffice
hearan hoo an acronym –
a D & C – wad dae
tae waash awa
hir kebbit pearl

an lukean oot thi windie
at a white plastic bag
risin past oor
second storey,
a flinricken escapin.

4

Here wiz thi sentence, then:
thi three, ma pearlie, and
wan mair simple daith,
his reid refusal tae be held –
gin ut wiz a he –
past mair nor a week o wir kennan:

yirdit: earthed; *flee's-wing*: very small or short; *kelder*: womb; *kebbit*: stillborn; *flin-ricken*: a weak person, very thin cloth, a mere rag.

mebbe ut wiz
a refusal tae be kent
lyk God's refusal tae prevent
thon previous collision
arrehvin in thi Haugh o Urr
atween meh car
an a jenny-wren:

sae sma a plosive
set this up
by silencin that sang,
sae haurd tae ken
God means yi as
His punctuaishun.

5

Sae licht thi lives that laive us
oor griefs maun growe insteed;
thi anely wean
a man can cairry's
absence inniz heid.

But leese me oan thi lea-laik-gair
that spelt me oot this speech,
thi sma hills o thi Stewartry
sae saftly preach
Eh nearly nivir heard yir nemm
i thi burr o ilka bee;

but ken noo that ut is your breist
Eh'm liggin oan tae listen.
Ut is your braith
that blaws thi feathirs o thi wurds
by me and awa.

---

leese me oan: an expression of preference; *lea-laik-gair*: the place where two hills
join together and form a kind of bosom; *burr*: a whirring noise as made in the throat
in pronouncing the letter 'r'; *liggin*: lying.

Lammer Wine

Is there onywan wha hisna stude
oan a heich cliff's edge and no begood
tae waant tae faa? Thi fatal mood
      is in us aa:
ye need nae Dante's mid-life wood
      tae hear uts caa.

Oor dwaums o flyin haud debate
wi common sense that sic a fate
is hailly negative a state
      and no release:
wha kens whit thochts sic draps create
      o dreid or peace?

Ye're shairly shair that when ye crash
thi rocks ablow will mak wan mash
o banes an brains an livin's fash:
      is that relief?
Thi fullest freedom in wan flash,
      yir best belief?

Or it ut unshared space tae fold
yir secrets in lyk leaf o gold,
demarkin whit cannot be told
      wi fufty foot:
yir scream thi gleid that's niver sold,
      yir aural loot?

Cast back yir harns lyk herrin nets
frae cliffs, no boats, tae whaur thi frets
an sulk o faem collects, furgets
      aa trace o pen;
ink blinks, and paper pulps; wet lets
      gae o mere men.

Lammer wine: amber wine, an imaginary liquor esteemed a sort of liquor of immortality (here associated with heather ale); *heich*: high; *begood*: begun; *dwaums*: dreams; *fash*: trouble; *gleid*: gleam; *harns*: minds; *faem*: foam; *tint*: lose.

Thi sea's whaur narratives gae blind
and sangs are jugged and stories brined,
whaur saga-wurms stert tae unwind:
            thi sea's thi place
whaur gin ye tint track o yir mind
            ye'll find yir face.

Can you no mind when Ireland's king
wiz crehd *Ard-righ*, when Niall did bring
his hostages tae hae a fling
            in Gallowa,
and nane o thi nine wad even sing
            his blues awa?

Sune Niall got bored wi slauchtrin Picts,
socht ither weys tae get his kicks;
nae hostage harpist pleyed 'im licks
            and sae thi think
crossed Ireland's brain: these Picts hae tricks
            wi makin drink.

Ye've mebbe clean forgot thi tale
o hoo thi Picts brewed heather ale;
ye mebbe caa yirsel a Gael
            o Irish line,
and sae dae thi inventors fail
            o Lammer wine.

Let keests o malts gae chalky-blank,
let magic mushrooms choke yir stank,
let willin partners huv a wank –
            they can't compare:
thi sowels that huvnae this drink drank
            ur chewin air.

---

heather ale: drink brewed from heather, the secret of making which was popularly
supposed to have been lost with the Picts (see the *Carmina Gadelica*, also R.L.
Stevenson's ballad *Heather Ale*); *keests*: tastes; *stank*: drain.

NOTE: *Niall Noigallach* was an early High King (*Ard-righ*) of Ireland. Five of his
nine hostages were from Ireland, four from Scotland. He campaigned in Galloway
towards the end of the fourth century AD.

Gin Burns hud anely hud wan drink
his statues warld-wide at wan wink
wad print oot rantin crambo-clink
      in standirt habbie:
twa centuries wad turn delinq-
      uent as deid Rabbie.

A Calvinist wad deselect
his mither frae amang thi Elect;
auld Hume wad sell his intellect
      fur jist wan drap –
thi baby Jesus wad neglect
      His mither's pap.

This isnae jist some siccar liquor,
this yill yince medd thi angels bicker
and stilled thi universe's ticker:
      nae warld wad spin
till wan sip, makin God's throat slicker,
      gar'd aa begin.

This wiz thi yill that Niall did seek
amang thi burnin corses' reek,
a culture instantly antique
      and rendirt null;
whaur livin Picts were quite unique
      intil thi Mull.

Wan faimly there alane steyed sapple,
thi wimmen tho hud cut thir thrapple;
twa sons, wan faither, kept thi apple
      o Lammer wine:
ahent a ditch nae force could tapple
      they waulked thi line.

crambo-clink: doggerel; *standirt habbie*: the stanza in which this poem is written; *yill*: ale; *Mull*: the Mull of Galloway, the southernmost tip of an archipelago in the extreme south-west of Scotland, reached across a narrow strip of land: it consists of high pasture surrounded by cliffs; *sapple*: supple, alive.

And fur a week auld Niall threw lives
as meaninfu as oors oan knives
that chapped them quick as wives chap chives
   an geed nae quaarter,
until they were by hunger's drives
   reducet tae barter.

'Gee me thi recipe,' said Niall,
'and breathe.' He thocht this a fair deal
considrin thi amoont o steel
   he'd brocht tae bear;
thi Pechties promptly seemed tae kneel
   an nicely swear.

But then thi story thickens, growes
as strange as aa thi separate vows
thae three men tuke: fur wan carouse,
   thi furst son said,
Eh will extract thi secret. Rouse
   me when Eh'm dead,

thi second claimed, Eh'll still sey nocht.
Wan o meh bairns'll no be bocht,
thi faither said, ye'll ne'er learn ocht
   frae thi tither;
kill wan, Eh'll whisper whit ye've socht
   intil his brither.

And thus wiz Pictish honour kept,
or sae Niall thocht, fur when he'd nipped
wan life thi tearless faither crept
   close tae thi brink,
and gripped his loose-moothed son and slipped
   intil thi drink.

Pechties: Picts.

24

And sae some cultures niver scrieve
thir myths doon sae whit we believe
aboot them's neither shoot nor sheaf
            o richt or wrang;
they gang doon wrecked oan history's reef
            withoot a sang.

And micht this no be lyk a purpose,
tae hint that silence sall usurp us
aa: gin we fecht ut'll Wyatt Earp us
            intae deid Clantons;
oor anely chance thi wey o thi porpoise:
            be pillie wantons.

Jist sae Niall sent ayont thi Pale
 thi recipe fur heather ale
till anely those prepared tae sail
            past sanity
will toast frae sic a brutal grail
            humanity.

And sic a keltie nane taks aff
wha kenna that they are time's chaff
whas tragedies wad gar God laugh
            gin He hud humour,
but He finds culture kinna naff
            an time a tumour.

But dinna doot He loves us aa
an didnae like tae see us faa
wrang-fittit by thi serpent's baa,
            He's still concedin:
haund heather ale owre til thi Law,
            we're back in Eden.

pillie wanton: the phrase appears in William Dunbar's *Of a Dance in the Quenis Chalmer*, David Daiches has described it as untranslatable; *keltie*: toast.

The Postcards of Scotland

My country is being delivered repeatedly
onto the 'WELCOME' mat of my mind
with the light patter of postcards falling
like flattened raindrops; postcards from
its every moniply, its each extremity:
the drunk dog's profile of Fife,
the dangling penis of Kintyre,
the appendix of the Mull of Galloway,
the uvula of Ulva and the sputum and
spat-out dentures of the Western Isles,
the whale's maw of the Moray Firth
and the steam-snort cockade
of the Orkneys.
                    Every village sends me
its image like a sweetheart's *Vergissemienicht*,
to be carried in the wallet on
a dangerous journey,
for I am voyaging so far within
all thoughts of 'home',
it is as though I were stationary, and
it is they who fly away in every direction;
Scotland exploding like a hand-grenade until
its clachans catch up with the stars,
its cities collide with galaxies, scattering
the contents of their galleries, unspooling
their cinemas, bargain-basketing
their shopping precincts.

Only their postcards survive,
like the familiarity of light
still travelling from extinguished stars.

But what postcards can endure transmission
across such addressless gulfs, insertion
in such a black hole as
the letterbox of my discrimination?

Certainly the tartan-fringed idylls
of small dogs and pretty girls
hypnotised by the contents of a flapping kilt
despite the rubicund obesity of its owner
and the fact he wears his gingery beard
sans moustache:
                    nothing shall destroy
these, not even the incendiary glance
of the Angel of Death,
for which reason Auld Clootie sends him them
weekly, along with their sib,
the fishermen catching Nessie,
because Auld Nick kens weel this degradation
of Thor's mythic encounter with
the Midgard Serpent
is a pain in the angelic butt.

But these I throw aside negligently
in the search for my true home.

Not the misty lomond monstrosities
of quality pap-merchants, with
their dug-up zombie shots, their same old
purpling panoramas of hills and lochs
giving the glad eye in weathers that never were.
Nor the shampooing of sheep and the oiling
of Highland cattles' horns; nor
the photographic humping of Belties
and the image-maker's posing hand
fist-fucking the cute black bun. Nor
the fascinating 'Doors of Many Post Offices' shot,
presenting such a quaint contrast
to the work of Bernhard und Hilla Becher
with series of urban water towers,
or the disused mines' pit-heads of Sanquhar,
and the lowland belt across to Fife.
Nor the orange and viridian 'Closes of Glasgow' series,
each tile personally signed
by Rennie Mackintosh, miraculously free
of asbestosis-tinged alcoholics' vomit.

Give me the postcards of municipal Scotland;
each caravan park lovingly identified
by a zen-succinct description printed
on a white border along the postcard's base:
each children's playpark accurately defined
down to the lack of smiles on the weans' faces;
each council flowerbed pointlessly recorded.
Here are the proud wastes of our city centres
accurately seen for the first time,
begotten from the copulation
of councillors with cement-mixers,
the tight wads of backhanders jammed
up their quivering rectums.

Here is the genuine face of eternity,
where 'swimming pool' means
a kidney-shaped pond eighteen inches deep,
the colour of chopped jobbies
full of pale bodies and pink flotation aids;
where 'beach' is a silver fingernail,
clipped and spinning from the camera like
a boomerang covered in lice.
Observe the two old men leaning towards
the water, out of focus; they
are transfixed by a monster more fecund
than any Nessie: that brown weasel shape
is a wet spaniel bitch,
you have only to scratch
the postcard to release the perfume
of soggy dog. Observe
that child on the sliver of toe-cheese
called the 'beach' at Portpatrick:
she has one foot in a plastic bucket
forever. Paradise smells
of tarry seaweed, it tastes of sand
in lettuce and tomato sandwiches.
I couldn't think of never dying
anywhere else.

Here is my only home,
my Heaven; observe
these photographs of Mercat crosses
and town centres packed with Anglias,
the ghosts of Hillman Minxes.
Surely those figures eating fried egg rolls
behind the glass of Italian cafés
are the philosophers of the Enlightenment.
Surely that is Susan Ferrier gossiping
outside the crappy dress shop
with Margaret Oliphant. Surely
Robert Burns is buying a haggis supper
from that chipper in Annan,
William Dunbar is stotting from
The Cement-Mixer's Arms.

Only in these images do I recognise
the beautiful nincompoop face
of my nation: the sullen brows
of the stultified young farmer
speeding out of shot;
the *Sweetheart Stout* expression
of the girl with a knife in her handbag.
Only in these postcards
can I ever be at rest.

The Horse of Blood

Can you no hear
meh hert's hooves clap
oan the coabbles ootben
yir farawa windie thi nicht?

Pu awa, ma dear,
thae sheets that hap
yir sleepin ear, an then
cwa tae thi gless wi a licht.

Dae you no see
thi cuddie o bluid
that's champan i thi street
ablow yir foreign bed thi nicht?

Come doon, *mo chree*,
he's slee, but guid,
he'll bear yi safe an fleet
as by yir luvir as thocht micht.

hap: cover; *cwa*: come away; *cuddie*: horse; *ablow*: below; *mo chree* (Gaelic): my darling; *slee*: sly; *by*: near.

The Empty Crow

Thi difference
atween
a hoodie preenin
i thi wind
and
a black polythene
bag, flappin oan
a fence
is no as big
as thon atween
ma past
an present tense
o thi weelkent phrase
'I love you'.

Thi furst
hud fleesh
near eneuch tae keest
thi second's learnin
hoo dear
distance
maks yir maik
hoo toom
aa muvement is
that taks ma hert
nae closer til
uts love.

atween: between; *hoodie*: hooded crow; *weelkent*: familiar, hackneyed; *eneuch*:
enough; *keest*: taste; *maik*: equal; *toom*: empty.

The Informationist's Love Song
(for Debbie)

Imagine a brazier topped with roasting chestnuts.
One of these chestnuts contains
the Prince of Denmark having a bad dream.
There are other princes in the other nuts:
of Bolivia, Nepal, Ruritania, and elsewhere.
Imagine thrusting your hand into these hot chestnuts
and drawing forth Hamlet, unscathed.
That is the likelihood of our meeting in this life.
(If you imagine yourself as the prince,
then you are Sarah Bernhardt,
and you must decide whether
you are pre-wooden leg or post- .)

My love for you attacks me with the persistence
of a hive of bees disturbed recently
by a tree surgeon in Darwin, Australia.
Stranded up a platform, he died after receiving
one thousand stings. Each of these stings is,
figuratively, a small arrow from
the countless quivers of a cloud of Cupids.
These pursue me round and round
the pedestal on which I would have placed you,
had they not assailed me with
a thousand instances of your loveliness.

Such instances as the nervous way you wink at me
during awkward moments in company;
or the abstracted manner in which one hand plays
with long strands of your hair, as
though you had forgotten how to plait it;
or how you always finish a bath
by rolling onto your belly and
sticking your small heels into the air.
These impress themselves upon me
with the resonance of misprinted phrases like
'those magnificent biros filled me with awe',
or the sign 'DEOORANTS' in Safeways in Penrith.

My love envelops you as benignly as
a bath filled with tomato soup
envelops someone sprayed with skunk-oil.
Total saturation is the only thing
which will remove the awful stench.
Just so my love removes past instances
of stinking behaviour by other men.

Inevitably the presence of the loved one
in each other's life acts as
the irritant in a mussel which produces the pearl.
I speak as one who walks beside the Tay,
'Europe's largest fresh water river system'
(*The Herald*, 13.2.93), which still sustains
one pearl fisherman. The colour and
therefore the value of the pearl depends
on where it is located within
the misshapen mussel: near the rim
it will be brown, further in yellow,
and at the heart white.
Such pearls are still called, in what is perhaps
a remnant of the vanished culture of the Picts,
the tears of the water god.

I would be to the great river of your heart
as the nineteenth-century worthy
George Farquharson was to the Tay.
He would walk around Perth wearing a hat
which stated 'Pearl Fisher to the Queen'.

The Ballad of the Hermit Crab

Ither craturs' hames Eh find
which they hae barely left ahind
afore Eh craa intae their rooms
as robbers scaffed in pharaohs' tombs.

Thir corses micht be elsewhaur derned,
thir waas and cots are mine unearned:
aa thi collogue o thi sea
they niver kent is heard by me.

Tae fit sae snod, sae trig and weel,
meh sowel maun be made o geal
forbye meh legs are peens that stab,
meh claas are shairp as houlet's gab.

When ilka hame at last growes sma,
Eh smoor ma fire and crack uts waa,
And syne wi stanes Eh intromit
till Eh can mak meh munelicht flit.

Nae laird can sic as me evict,
Eh grup as Scot and dree as Pict:
aside yir firths, inside yir speak,
Scotland is the shell Eh seek.

scaffed: grubbed around to see what they could find; *corses*: bodies; *collogue*: whispered conversation; snod, trig: neat, proper; *geal*: jelly; *forbye*: howsoever; *peens*: pins; *claas*: claws; *houlet*: owl; *smoor ma fire*: ritual damping down of the domestic fire at night; *intromit*: conduct business; *munelicht flit*: removal of one's household at night to avoid paying debts; *dree*: endure; *speak*: language.

HIT THE NORTH

'Concepts are "autopoetic" entities, defined not by their referential relations to other things or states of affairs but by the relations between their elements as well as their relations to other concepts.'

PAUL PATTON

explicating Gilles Deleuze

'Gin ye hidna been amon the craws ye widna hae bin shot.'

Speak o' the North-East

ed. William Morrice Wilson

Why the Elgin Marbles Must Be Returned to Elgin

Because they are large, round and bluey,
      and would look good on the top of Lady Hill.
Because their glassy depths would give local kids
      the impression that they are looking at
      the Earth from outer space.
Several Earths in fact, which encourages humility
      and a sense of relativity.
Because local building contractors would use
      JCBs to play giant games in Cooper Park
      and attract more tourists to Morayshire:
      'Monster Marble Showdown Time!'
Because the prophecy omitted from the Scottish Play
      must be fulfilled:
      'When the marbles come back to Elgin
      the *mormaer* will rise again.'
(A *mormaer* being a Pictish sub-king.
Which Macbeth was, not a thane.
Nor a tyrant, for that matter.
More sort of an Arthur figure, you know,
      got drunk and married Liza Minelli, with
      Gielgud as Merlin the butler.)
Because they're just gathering dust
      sitting in the British Museum, never mind
      the danger that if someone leans against them
      they might roll and squash a tourist like a bug.
Because the Greeks, like the rest of Europe,
      don't know where Scotland is, and so
      won't be able to find them.
Because if they come looking we can just
      push the marbles into the Firth off Burghead
      and show them the dolphins instead.
Greeks like dolphins. Always have.
Because it will entertain the dolphins
      watching the Elgin marbles roll with the tides
      and perhaps attract whales.

Because whales can balance the marbles
    on the tops of their spouts,
    then ex-Soviet tourist navies can come
    and fire big guns at them
    like in a funfair.
Because the people of Morayshire were
    originally Greek anyway, as proven by
    Sir Thomas Urquhart in his *Pantochronochanon*.
And by the fact they like dolphins.
Because we are not just asking for them,
    we demand their return, and this
    may be the marble that sets the heather
    alight, so to speak.
Because if the Stone of Destiny is
    the MacGraeae's tooth, then
    the Elgin marbles are
    the weird sisters' glass eyes.
Because Scotland must see visions again,
    even if only through
    a marble of convenience.

Roadkill

That summer I kept hitting gulls
off the top of my windscreen
like breasting a white-hatted wave
as I sped down the country roads:
herring gulls mainly, and
their brown-speckled young,
bulky birds all, that
looking in my mirror I'd see
drop, vertically, from
an already distant impact point,
and smack upon the tarmac.

Roadkill had been bad that year:
I kept passing smears of pheasant,
well-parted rabbits' ears,
the odd pigmy mammoth, hunched by
the verge, malnourished,
obviously dead, and
various eohippi.

On the road to Buckie one blustery day
when the sun tried bursting out
of hill-big rain-clouds, I saw
a series of creatures, half-squid, half-skate,
pale and lurid in that orangey light,
too battered to identify.

Gradually my small white car began
to alter: a membrane-like look
crept over the bumpers
as of a seabird's foot;
the hint of a pale eye glinted back
from the side mirror.
Once as I drove along
the undulant lane to Lhanbryde,
there was a rippling off the bonnet
as of feathers in a fierce breeze.

After the fifteenth gull
the seats seemed to be covered in shagreen,
a seaweed smell came off the wheel
onto my hands, and
there was an isinglass flash
to the windows.

Obviously, the car, under the impact of
so many souls, had begun to adapt.
I started slipping whitebait in
the petrol tank as a treat,
visiting the coast nightly, until
an angel of the sandstone cliffs by Burghead
told me what to do.

That night, having strewn the back seat
with haddock and tangles, I drove
to the end of Grant Street, that looks
past the Pictish fort to the Firth,
and there asperged the dashboard
with fifteen year-old Ordiequish.
Slipping the car into first I drove,
door open, past the last houses, lighter in my lap.

Just before the drop
I jumped, dropping the flame:
the fire quickly filled the interior
with a flicker of white wings
as the car hit the dark waters.
I watched it tumble and sink
the fifteen feet or so to liberty.

Ode to Scotty

We kent ut wiz yir accent that
they couldna tak much mair o –
thae engines – foarmed somewhaur atween
Belfast and Ontario.

O Mister Scott, weel may ye talk
aboot WARP Factor Seven:
you tuke thi clash o Brigadoon –
transpoartit ut tae Heaven.

But still we luve ye tho ye werr
a Canuck in disguise:
tho Spock an Banes baith fanciet Kirk
you luved thi Enterprise.

Noo that we aa could undirstaund
fur ilka Scoatsman dotes
oan engines – see hoo Clydesiders
still bigg thir wee toy boats.

An syne therr wiz yir pash fur booze
fae Argyle tae Arcturus;
ye ootdrank Klingons grecht an smaa –
anither trait no spurious.

We kent dilithium crystals werr
(tho in thir future foarm)
thi semm gems that ye find gin you
crack stanes aroond Cairngorm.

An whit a bony fechtir, eh?
Sae martial a revure,
while Kirk left you in oarbit fur
three-quaartirs o an oor

clash: conversation, local speech; *ilka*: each; *bigg*: build; *syne*: then; *gin*: if; *revure*:
a look of calm scorn or contempt.

while he an Spock an Banes plunked aff
tae some furbidden planit –
ye kent they werr oan lusty splores
but still ye birled lyk granite.

But maist o aa we luve ye coz
ye saved oor naishun's fiss:
ye nivir whinged aboot Englan but –
ye beat thum intae Space!

plunked aff: played truant; *splores*: jaunts, antics; *birled*: spun.

The Third Corbie

1

I have seen the third corbie,
the one who doesn't speak
but is always riding away
down the straight lanes by
Thornhill and Clackmarras on
his bicycle made of dead men's bones
with a skull for a rattling bell.

2

The third corbie doesn't speak
with the raw black voice
of other crows; his beak
is full of soot
which trickles from it as
he murmurs to himself
the names of the dead you think
you would have liked to meet.

3

Today I watched the third corbie and
the grey horse nod respectfully
to one another outside my window,
the grey trying all the while to stifle
a jet plane whinny
he can see approaching from
the back of his cloud-free skull,
while the third corbie rubs
his ruefully hoof-remembering arse.

4

The third corbie has
a soft poke full of blue knights' eyes
like boilings
which he weighs abstractedly
on seeing a child.

5

The third corbie plays
the zither, squatting in a splayed-
out tree. There is
no chain on his bicycle, which back
spins its pedals idly as it leans
against the trunk, remembering when
it was a few good men.

As you approach him thankfully
he is always in
the farther away tree.

6

No one has ever stolen
the bicycle of the third corbie
twice, or so
the poor bones say
and they should know.

7

The third corbie has
been thrown out of the parliament of crows
for purveying a blend
of stout and cough linctus to the young.
I watch his stoned victims fall
from the trees of the Linkwood road
like large plums
and burst in feathers and pith
on the dry-tongued tarmac.

8

I would love to talk to you
for days and years and soon
will never have done so I find
my mouth is saying
to the third corbie
who cycles away.

9

Hours later when there is
no trace of the third corbie
this monstrous whinny erupts
from the grey horse outside my window
like the lagging roar
of a silent fighter.

10

The bell
on the third corbie's bike
could not really be said to tinkle;
it's more a small knocking note
like beetles in a rafter:
fnoc fnoc fnoc

11

The third corbie is
large and expressively lit
as he cycles round Moray merrily
rattling his eyeless bell away
through the blue sewers of
the jet-polluted air:
fnoc fnoc fnoc

12

The other night I woke
from a wintry dover to find
I'd spilled my whisky on
the third corbie.
He silently climbed in my red-eyed fire
and shook the Longmorn from his feathers
then crawled out, roasted
nude as a baby with drumstick limbs
and stared at me.

dover: nap.

44

13

I'd love to talk with you
for days and years and soon
will never have done, I said
to the third corbie
in the comfort and delight
of my own rented home,
but the hour is late
and I must get away.

Corbandie

See thi corbie oan thi wire
i thi bullyragglan wund
wi a braichum up o feathirs roond'iz heid:

syne he pints intil thi blast
lyk a collie oan thi brae
at thi cloods that split lyk sheep aboot'iz neb;

syne he stauchers, steps, and flauchters
till he dips his heid an grips:
ut's as near's he gets tae flehan oan thi spot.

But he wullna let ut gae
an be breeshilt by thi breeze
tho ut gees um coordy-licks wi aa uts micht,

till thi meenut that he waants tae,
syne thon burd wull spang thi lift
lyk a fleck o ess that's fleean up thi lum.

An sae ut'll be wi you, ma luve,
an thi bairn in yir wame
i thi hanlawhile that lichters you o hur;

fur therr's naebody sall ken
o thi cause that maks hur cry
'Here comes in corbandie' – an be boarn.

Corbandie: *corbandie*: in argument, some great difficulty which opposes a plausible hypothesis; *corbie*: a raven; *bullyragglan*: noisy, abusive wrangling; *braichum up*: an untidy wrapping up against the weather; *stauchers*: staggers; *flauchters*: flutters; *breeshilt*: rustled, hurried; *coordy-licks*: blows to incite one to fight; *spang*: leap elastically; *ess*: ash; *lum*: chimney; *wame*: womb; *hanlawhile*: short space of time; *lichters*: delivers.

The Horse Outside: *anaa*: as well; *clarty*: muddy; *pows*: foreheads; *yett*: gate; *reek*: smell; *howdie*: midwife; *thi ae*: the same.

The Horse Outside

Thi horse ootside
ma windie wiz
broon and white;
a piebald mare
thi colour o pubs
and hospitals.

When ut whinnied
Eh wiz convinced
wir bairn wad be
a horse anaa
Eh kent ut like
thi back o ma neck.

Thi horse ootside
wiz thi colour o whisky
and thi clarty white car
Eh'd drehv ye tae
Maternity in
i thi blond Mairch licht.

When ut nicht-galloped
uts hooves wad drum
lyk heavy nails
upon wir pows
and thi bairn wad kick
at thi yett o yir wame.

Gin thi horse's reek
and slang o thi Spey
made aa thae malts
whit shid Eh dae
wi thon Aiberdeen gull
and uts echo, meh dochtir?

When thi howdie said
'This is hoo strang
contractions shid be,'
hoo did Eh ken
they were thi ae strength
that aathin's at?

Kimmerin

Hoo lang werr ye born
or at aa? Ut wiz mornin,
we werr in thi grey hoose
up thi track fae Clackmarras.
Eh'd jist got in ma car
when Eh saw thi hare
i thi side mirror
o ma still-open door.

Ma dawtie, Eh froze;
thi car wiz a tortoise
ut waantit ti race.
Fae field's edge tae gress
uts grey stilt legs
emerged, and ut began
tae overtake slowly
uts auldest foe.

An this wiz yir kimmerin;
sae nearly simmer
Eh remembir Eh thocht,
as Eh sat and waatcht
ut entir thi field
o thi horses, o thi bield
o heich wheat ut'd appeared fae
that wiz thi colour o yir hair.

kimmerin: an entertainment at the birth of a child; dawtie: darling; bield: protection, safe place.

August in the Laich

Thi thistledoon blaws ower thi land
lyk thi sillery ghaists o bees
whispran in a green lug here
an gaithrin therr
in a foggy clyre o gressis.

Thi thistledoon blaws ower
thi bonny blond mains o Morayshire
and ower
thi last o thi harebells i thi lanes
an thi purpie spires
o rose-bay willa herb
an thi yella o thi tansy and
thi mimulus that derns thi burn.

Thi thistledoon blaws ower thi Aagust parks
till thi cuddies come at a rin and hoast
i thir ain kickd-up doost
an thi blue hills beek ayont thi Firth.

Thi thistledoon blaws an drifts
an aa uts message is:
'nae messages, nae messages...'
Thi wheat shirrs i thi breeze
an pints thi wey thi news is gauin.

clyre: diseased gland, cluster; *derns*: conceals; *hoast*: cough drily; *beek*: bask; *shirrs*: moves together.

Becoming Joseph

Becoming Joseph is unbecoming Jesus. Christ.
Becoming Joseph is agitating the sacred rat
    in the chest cavity cartwheel.
Is staring in the mirror beneath fluorescent light
    at the prairies of your scalp beneath
    the tumbleweed of your thinning hair.
Becoming Joseph in this instance is passing
    between the ages of thirty-three
    and thirty-four which is like passing from BC
    to AD.
Is stepping from the welded circle of recurrences,
    tablecloth-maps of Ireland, Wales, and card games,
    Newmarket, Stop the Bus, steak pie New Years,
    faces ageing too slowly to see, small rooms
    experiencing slight shrinkage from
    the time you can't remember first
    being carried into them, big as temples, to
    their present dimensions as boxes containing
    unworn and unnecessary slippers.
The faces commented on your wisdom concerning dinosaurs.
Much drawing on the backs of Christmas cards ensued.
A volume on the Mau Mau was removed from the sideboard.
Becoming Joseph is stepping onto the receding prairies
    where throat cancer trees surround
    snarled haemorrhoidal oases, where
    blackened furniture is broken through the sand
    like the spokes of Pharaoh's chariot wheels,
    where the china from cabinets like sunken clippers
    is broken like shells you crush underfoot
    but there is no sea, the cousins wail,
    no sand-coated cones, no White Coons,
    no sewage pipes, no Fifies.
Relatives pocket here and there,
    tribes missing, the ark missing, Moses missing,
    Mount Sinai missing – such a large hill,
    you hoped it might remain in sight.
Becoming Joseph is recoiling from AD to BC,
    becoming one of the lost bunches that made
    their cockeyed way to Pictland,
    neither chosen nor elect.

What can Joseph believe, after all? The angel
   did not come for him and could not.
Easier to flee back to Egypt, enter the realm
   of justifying his own child, carrying
   the beloved supplanter on his baffled back,
   to enter the antechamber of his own tomb,
   coterminous with the world,
   to sit there with the dust in his fists.
You'd like to pack the infant into a talking capsule,
   fire it off towards some planet that turns
   out in fact to still be here, only a
   few miles in the future, but
becoming Joseph is understanding you didn't
   walkabout the waste, build the rocket,
   write the book, to protect the child,
   but because the angel couldn't speak to you.
The relatives huddle like coathangers and daleks
   in the next room in the desert,
   watching everything they used
   to feed and sustain themselves become primitive,
   more ancient with each touch.
   fork becoming spoon becoming scoop becoming horn.
They turn themselves by the turbines becoming
   mill-wheels of their own breaths into
   their ancestors, put on names and faces
   they only remember from the photographs,
   find only polished bronze
   to stare in, become people whose histories
   no one knows, especially them,
   whose mouths are unable to provide
   information too different to comprehend.
Becoming Joseph is lying down in the cold night
   of the dogshit desert with the moon
   pushing your ear into the grains,
   staring into hour after hour of sand
   until you see each particle is
   a blinded face you seem to recognise.
Then you've certifiedly become Joseph, sitting there
   with a fist filled with your fathers' dust,
   a fist filled with all your mothers,
   watching your child dance to some tune
   you can't hear any more but know
   will eventually drive him, drive her, here.
You've become Joseph.

Looking Up from Aeroplanes

Do you too soon forget the brown
frownland far below,
between the slippery blotchings of
cloud-shadows, the
zip-fasteners of farm-lanes,
the telephone pad-hatchings of the towns
and look up?
        Into
that darkening of the blue
through the occasional vapour trail
like a larval tubule to
the grainy upper layers
grazed thin by stubbly cheeks,
the sore lips of peering
angels,
        each one packed together with
the others like white fish,
touching each other and
the whole sky at every point raised
by their massive iris
whose pupil is the blinded sun.

DOWN IN THE SOUTH

'The most efficient oppressor is the one who persuades his underlings to love, desire and identify with his power; and any practice of political emancipation thus involves that most difficult of all forms of liberation, freeing ourselves from ourselves.'

TERRY EAGLETON

'You see, my dear, you have fallen in to the dopiness of your surroundings.'

W.S. GRAHAM

The Lawn in Winter

is thinking hard. It was lain
in the shape of Scotland, now
it's been edged to a female torso.

It knows it is made of
turf rectangles which once
were folded over like thick

books. That would make
the lorry it came in like
a library. It knows

such things, but can't imagine
the field it came from. It
can't remember the weight

of cattle, and fantasises
it was stolen from a famous
Scottish golf course.

It would smile at the faces
of those early morning golfers
but it hasn't got a head.

Much of the Western Highlands
have now been covered
in clover. Dandelions root

like nipples over Aberdeen.
The frost does not discriminate
between its regions.

One time it snowed:
this aided concentration.
The lawn wants to know

when it began: was it when
its different editions
started to knit? Or when

the population arrived in
hard casings? (The ladybirds,
it decides, were volkswagens.)

Was it the first massacre
when the Mower of the Scots
made it suffer in strips?

Or was it the weight of women's
breasts pressing into it
all summer? It could take

months to sort this out.

Ballad of the King's New Dialect

When Jamie ran to London toon
tae tak up his new throne,
he drapped his pack o playin bards
wi jist thi wan 'Ochone'.

Fur he wiz noo thi Roses' king
and spak thi Roses' speak,
and kent nae mair thi Thistle's leid
than he did thon o thi Leek.

Though noo and then a traitrous burr
lyk bad wind could be whiffed
or sticky-wullie haein a cling
ontil a hizzie's shift.

Syne aa thi king's abandont crew,
his auld pleyed-oot Pleiades
did girn oan hoo pair Scots wiz deid
lyk fuitba-lossin laddies.

And wan or twa o them began
tae treh oan English laurels
which seemed a chic improvement oan
a cap o kail an sorrels.

There wiz wan doon-drag wi this speak;
that when they trehd tae spake ut,
though cleidit up in fustian dods
thir tongues still felt stark nakeit.

But naewan thocht tae waarn thi king
though ane and aa could hear ut;
thi English nobles foond ut fun,
thi Scots bards were too feart.

ochone: alas; *leid*: language; *sticky-wullie*: goose-grass; *hizzie*: hussy; *shift*: under-dress; *girn*: moan, complain; *doon-drag*: drawback; *cleidit*: swaddled; *dods*: garments.

Ye're thinkin: whas thi laddie then?
thi usual wan wha caas
oan seein thi king paradin past
'Eh speh thi royal baas!'

Insteid that pairt o Jamic's coort
frae Embro's landit clique
devestit utsel quite literally
and sae uts scions still streak.

Sune oor toons' puir began tae ape
this style they could afford
by tearin oot o thir urbane mous
ilka rural wurd.

And this is whit thi London lug
finds better than erotica –
thi anely 'haurd' word left is 'fuck':
narcoticised demotica.

Fur ivry Rabbi that proclaims
anither Booker Crisis
some Jockstrap's gettin stuffed wi cheques –
remember: pets win prizes.

Sae here's the chafe gin wan o us
frae Jamie's former *Heimat*
should think tae wear mair wurdy claes
in this appallin climate,

thi creh gaes up fae fowk roond here
'That jessie's wearin a jaiket!'
Gab's garb's aa inauthentic when
ut's casual tae gang nakeit.

jessie: effeminate male.

Dirty Drinking

Dirty drinker – n. *one who drinks alone*
and for the love of drinking.
CHAMBERS SCOTS DICTIONARY

What drives us to
think in public,
the miserable cornered few
in the happy bars?

Not looking good,
since that we seldom do
through the pitiless lens
of the satiated eye.

The perfect cynosure
makes more sure
their site's surrounded by
a hapless hungry stare.

So what? Light certainly,
smoke as incense and
the light, thick struts of it,
like a folded deckchair,

leaning on the lace
and nicotine of curtains.
Lucidity of tumblers
in Spring's warm snap;

that flash on rims,
this black tulip glass
standing in for a skull's
neat emptiness

at half past two
for those who will not speak,
not even to
the recognising barman,

that morbid crew.
Certainly preferring in the main
'the clear physical eye
against the erring brain'.

Absurd Canutes,
we should commute
to meditation halls
and bird calls

where light is like fish-stock
filling a glass ladle
and lain against floorboards
full of face-like knots,

to chambers full
of others' careful breaths
in the honest spool
and shrug of light.

But in my study's darkness too
this faint pressure to
prevent midnight
makes me conscious of

those other others cast beyond
the slant of moments,
like drunken deities, like
the dead, like angels

who fill in for emptiness,
that lovely stout,
on the many occasions
when our supply runs out.

And this is what stays
through the liquid days,
this greedy calmness, not
some urge to conquer thought,

but hoping in that brawl
of bar-room echoes to hear
one word of theirs
break this glass.

Ballad of a Failure

'Syne they came on to a garden green,
And she pu'd an apple frae a tree –
Take this for thy wages, True Thomas;
It will give thee the tongue that can never lie.'

The eighties were my Eildon Hills;
I flipped, I was dewigged:
I took the Queen of Elfland's pills,
for seven years I gigged

where no one but MacDiarmid went:
the dictionary's belly;
in dialects' intestines gave
it inauthentic welly.

The eighties were my Mexico,
my Denver and Tangiers;
I Ginsberged and I Kerouaced,
I Burroughsed down for years.

Scots was my junk, my doldrums were
Dundee and lack of cash;
I tried to sober up, write right,
I hid my language-stash.

I did the nineties thing back then,
too soon, and none too well;
the heteronyms, the Audenesques,
the paranoiac tale.

Then Graham-*slash*-O'Hara was
my far too strong precursor;
cubistic neo-ballads made
me a slacked-out non-discourser.

For seven years I tried to make
the abstract surface sing,
and never found a reader who'd
admit they'd heard a thing.

For seven years I only drank
with the jawless dirty dead:
Dunbar and Urquhart, Davidson –
True Thomas was our head –

and Soutar and MacDonald,
our Keats: poor Fergusson –
the sick, the senile and the mad
to me seemed hale and sane.

I never saw that country's queen –
I was too stoned to look;
too busy stalely loitering
to ever write a book.

I met someone (it happens) who'd –
at last – some commonsense;
she seized my workshy baseball bat
and smashed me through the fence

that separates this field from that
half-world of unrevision;
I married her, I published more,
I suffered decompression.

The nineties are my Tay roadbridge
as concrete as it gets
with so much Fairy Liquid in
the mix disaster waits.

Each pile is spined with skeletons –
the poets I've just listed –
my wife is pepper-feisty, but
the Tay is many-fisted.

The bridge is open either way,
while cash- and word-flow's smooth:
the nineties are my Ercildoune
and I must tell the truth.

Dog Conversion Chart

A poodle equals an empty bottle of vodka.

A corgi equals a Hillman Imp.

A cigarette equals a dog's anus.

An alsation equals the lung of a Martian.

Half a Yorkshire terrier equals a slipper.

An airedale equals hot spaghetti hoops.

A human leg equals Trixie, bitch-goddess of Lurv.

A West Highland terrier equals the beard of Da Vinci.

A tree equals a lamppost.

Ten trees equal the smell of a public library.

A Jack Russell equals a cat who gambles.

A woman's armpit, depending on whether it is shaven or
unshaven, equals various kinds of labrador.

Vomit equals meat and two veg.

A Red Setter equals Shepherd's Delight.

Lassie equals the love child of Elizabeth Taylor
and Montgomery Clift.

A seal equals a dog without legs that can fly.

A wolf equals the holy solitude of the drunk.

Ten wolves equal deep shit.

A pekingese equals a human face,
thrust forever into a human boot.

The Ballad of a Success

Come hear Glowbucket's sorry tale,
the Lit-boys' former darling,
from when he first peed in his pail
to his last recorded snarling.

He was their kind of bit of scruff:
he wrote – *and* played piano,
a college-free, wee London buff
who photod like Keanu.

He'd knock back stout as though it made
him Irish-ish by proxy,
and with his northern bluff conveyed
a southern orthodoxy.

His politics were radical –
for Islington, that is –
his mores were more lad_ical·
this combo wowed the press.

Abruptly rendered nearly-famous
by a critic's tender blow,
he shook hands with the nearly-Seamus:
his career was afterglow.

The first book was his best one
till his second, then his third;
his fourth one begged the question
'Do we need a new award?'

His fifth book, strangely, bombed;
by then no one could distinguish
his voice from the last one they'd acclaimed
for galvanising English.

He switched his style biannually,
he learnt those old dogs' tricks;
his publisher – quite cordially –
rejected volume six.

He now traversed the low road
where you and I still labour,
each lane so deeply furrowed
that none can see their neighbour.

He'd run into you in your trench
and whimper, 'Make it stop:
as soon as syntax...' – here he'd flinch –
'we go over the top!'

By volume nine the scene once more
acknowledged his existence,
and silently unlatched the door
inscribed 'For Your Persistence'.

At last he was a grand old thing –
at least in terms of age –
the writing was plain wittering,
but it still filled up the page.

So now he trains the latest pup
the proper ways to say –
old poets never do shut up,
they just pantoum away.

The Gift Horse

Mouth of mashed potato
smells of peat and shoe polish:
I could go walking on those gums
and climb among
the crashed sonatas of those teeth,
those nicotine precipices!

Soft fruits bruise across
the carse of that tongue,
rasps, strawberries, logans:
tayberries burst, blueberries smear.
It's raining sugar on
those rotten buds, those frostbite toes!

Mane made of proud women's hair
and the moustaches of editors
all of whom rejected you
again and again, but who now
claim interest, as though
a percentage made on your neglect!

Hooves of boiled-down books
bound with glue oozed
from ashtrays, hash, and
dreggy booze, shod
with the dream of future books
and stamped into your forehead!

Tail of cursed brush stubs,
of Tam o' Shanter's mare's
shit-bestreakit pluckings, grey
as the temples of failures
biting down on sarks
that covered former lovers' arses!

sarks: shirts.

Get Complex

So you wish to become invisible, a brother
    with ice and sleep, with the unwritten;
to be an extra on lost celluloid,
    to duck the pecking questionnaires
those sent fanatic by uncertainty
    cling to: all faux-ideologies?
You think that such societies exist,
    of preachers voluntarily
unlistened-to? And you suppose that I'm
    a member of this see-through sect,
St Oran's Order of the Buried Mouth?
    No need to swear: drink this; you're in.

We offer sanctuary to those exhausted
    by Aristotle's pilgrimage
from A to not-A and back, dittoed on
    nearly-erased kneecaps each day
by pi-ish politicians and the press.
    Humanity, technology,
is never merely good or bad – or worse:
    authentic or unnatural,
but somewhere in the greys our habits spread
    as the brain's best stab at rainbow.
Upon the mile from Paradise to Hades
    are Limbo's multivalent leas.

Dwelling near the equivocating angels
    and various pre-Socratics may
appear down-market in the holy stakes,
    but we are agents balancing
such whirlwinds as the end of history
    upon apocalyptic pins
and shaving them with razors that restore
    the fuzz beneath the slavered foam.
Don't vanish from simplicity's salons
    then, fade into its crude work, be
a sleeper in our incremental cells,
    await your wake-up code: *get complex!*

Because we must resist what we espouse,
    your mission, which you should refuse,
is to convert our love of futures back
    into that currency of dread
once common in deals with the numinous;
    because its strangeness must obscure
our patient deaths that wait within it at
    their always-primitive guns, if
we are to advance into its territory
    at all, that other century.
Since neither faith nor fact can shield us then
    we must learn how to disappear.

Smirr

The leaves flick past the windows of the train
like feeding swifts: they're scooping up small mouth-
fuls of the midge-like autumn, fleeing south
with the train's hot wake: their feathers are small rain.
'Serein' they could say, where I'm passing through,
then just a sound could link rain with the leaves'
symptom, of being sere. But who deceives
themselves such rhyming leaps knit seasons now?
Some alchemist would get the point at once;
why I, against the leaves' example, try
migrating to my cold roots like a dunce.
Thicker than needles sticking to a fir,
Winter is stitching mists of words with chance,
like smears of myrrh, like our small rain, our smirr.

HIT THE NORTH *(REMIX)*

'It was deemed that if something hadn't happened 30 seconds into the programme, viewers would change channels. They think 'Shit' and press the remote control *...click.* Now someone tells me it's eight seconds.'

PAULA MILNE

'Would you credit it?'

MARK E. SMITH

In Chips We Trust

As I sat on the Aberdeen train
mainlining *The Fugitive* through
a Video Walkman-thing thanks to
'Ironhorse Entertainment' (true) –
the first to sample
a trial run of this module,

I heard a sad refrain
engorge my black foam earphones,
a chorus of those spirits lost
in lardy Cyberlimbo,
plugged into games and laptops with
their frontal lobes akimbo:

'Brookside is my Sophocles
Noel is my Wilde,
the Bionic Man's my long-lost pa
and Sonic is my child:
so help my head
in microchips we trust.

The Street's my only Chekov
Steve Wright is my Swift,
the News at Ten is Mister Benn
and Prozac's babble's gift:
so help my head
in microchips we trust.

Neighbours is my opera
Eastenders is the troof,
Cath Beale has chopped mein dick off
and this shall be my proof:
so help my glans head
in microsurgery we trust.'

I watched my little Kimble run
from the cops with the copters,
the guys with the guns
into the web of intercoms,
computer link-ups, ID cards,
dam-high jumps, and glass door shards;

pantherine rozzers
and plods who were thick;
thought 'Dick be nimble,
Dick be quick...'
and knew I too must singalonga
this choral Phlegetelethona:

'Mister Chekhov is my Chekhov
Beadle's the eye of God,
send Palin through the Earth this time
my armchair will applaud:
*so help my head
in microchips we trust.*

Kirk is my Odysseus
Nature's my RSC
where the actors are turned to animals
and David is Circe:
*so help my Attenboroughs
in microchips we trust.'*

Then as we slid across the border,
hunter and prey were reconciled;
I hit the rewind button, watched the rammy
as Scotsmen, stern and wild,
ordered those damp cheeseburgers,
devoured those clammy
jam-injected junkie doughnuts,
each jaw declaring in its
own complicated code
of masticating morse
or saliva semaphore
their dedication to the cud.

I knew I had escaped
my video blindfold
only to arrive amang
a people cast into a similar cold:
the gut of gluttony, of which
Dunbar the makar sang.
I could be no more than a stitch
in this great beefy side,
but this is what I tried:

'Well may you wail, Caledonia, hame
o thi MacSlacker & thi Nanesaehip,
o thi mealie puddin & thi microwaveable chip:
it is to your televised fitbaa games
thi ee o oor soaffie-tattie turns,
it is fur you
oor triple-bypassed hert burns.

Land o the carbohydrate spree
whas political will
is aboot as clarified as ghee,
we dee fur thee still
i thi mini-Floddens o wir lobbies,
thi wee Cullodens o wir livin-rooms,
and whilst attemptin tae pass
fibre-free jobbies
through a pile-crooned ass,
we meet oor cholesterol-driven dooms.'

But even as I ended
this satire I intended
would see my nation mended
        or made humble,
my stomach, not offended,
        gave a grumble:

'Forget yir Immortal Rabbie
and his tricky Standirt Habbie:
gee me thi Standirt Haddie
        (Supper, of course),
bocht in the Ashvale, laddie,
        lyk thi heid o a horse.'

Forgive me my heart
in chips we trust.

'Forget yir Fuzzy Logic,
Pound's duties pedagogic,
forget thi gaudy magic
    o a guid Scots wurd:
your appetite huz tragic-
    ally demurred.'

Forgive me my heart
in chips we trust.

'A nano-sec's reflection
wid show ye the connection
atween the current predilection
    fur computers
and oor love o aa confection-
    ery that blooters.'

Forgive me my heart
in chips we trust.

'King Shit-Click shall rule o'er us
and aa wha thocht afore us
shall mystify and bore us
    fur that briefest blip,
till we aa jine in thi chorus:
    Maist Holy Chip!'

The Flock in the Firth

As Eh cam owre thi Forth rail brig
Eh saw frae oot o Fife
a farrachin o starlins, trig
as thi thochts o ane waukrife.

Lyk sheelock fae a thrashin mill
they mirlieit thi nicht
atween thi brigs, as tho tae fill ut
wi wan shammade o flicht.

Lyk a sark that's bealin i thi breeze
this ram stam scarnach oan
a norrie birled wi siccan ease
assa skatir by'ur lone.

Ut seemd as tho a michty scroosh
o sparlins fae thi flair
o Forth hud fur a skirr gaed whoosh
intil thi deeps o air.

Ut seemd as tho a page o wurds
at sum parafflin nemm,
had aa at wance been cheengd tae burds
an werr marginin thi faem.

Thi mirk held mair nor myriads
aa sherrickin thi stream,
in spirlin splores, in sklents, in scads,
lyk Hitchcock's wuddendreme.

---

farrachin: bustling; *waukrife*: unable to sleep; *sheelock*: chaff; *mirlieit*: speckled; *shammade*: lacework; *sark*: shirt; *bealin*: moving agitatedly; *ram stam*: headstrong; *scarnach*: great number of people or things; *norrie*: whim; *birld*: spun; *by'ur lone*: by herself; *scroosh*: disreputable horde; *sparling*: smelt (a freshwater fish found in the Forth and the Tay); *skirr*: jape; *parafflin*: flourishing, as at the end of a signature; *marginin*: marking the margin; *mirk*: dark; *sherrickin*: amassing to abuse; *spirlin splores*: lively excursions; *sklents*: angles; *scads*: in great quantities; *wuddendreme*: nightmare.

Lyk Egypt's *kas*, or Dante's braw
adulterers in Hell,
sae mony starlins i thi blaw
o Scoatlan rose an fell.

Eh slid ablow thi skavie flock
and oantae Fife's blank page,
Eh wrote: they are thi parrymauk
o starnies inna rage.

skavie: rushing; *parrymauk*: double; *starnies*: stars ('starn' also means 'starling').

Song of the Terrible Lizard

1

Hoarse as the alien music that you hear
pour from dry toilet taps on speeding trains
the dinosaur encouched in my back-brain
told me about her dreams. She was, she claimed,
a classic case: Triassic period
extinction complex. This meant detailed nightmares
of barking modems, multinational soup-
sud corporations, and commuters filled
with marge: all small-mammalian-run.
My sympathy for the reptile was wasted;
she didn't want the pity of a figment
from her sleep's future. Go on, ask me how
you psychoanalyse a fossil. No?
Few want to listen to their lizard's tongue,
still less acknowledge that they understand
the feelings of the dead. Our population's
a saurian humunculus: its bulk
lies hip-high in the mulch-fields of the south,
its spindle-neck ascends to granite crops
and northern muirs – I simply put my ear
to Loch Ness's peat-discoloured depths to see
what I could hear. Of course Diplodocus
has two brains, one lodged tight in pelvic London,
the other little more than acorn-sized,
plopped in silt somewhere on the black loch floor.
But which does all the dreaming, can you guess?
Yes: miles from real digestion, of Kultur
or Kapital, the minikin mind waits
in Scotland for slow signals rising with
the latest gut reaction. Just to pass
the time, you realise, it prophesies
similar cataclysms to its own
meteor-borne doom; viruses and eating
disorders loom large in its nut-sized cortex.

2 The Ballad of Techofear

'The fossil looked at me and winked.
It's rather fun to be extinct.'
OGDEN NASH

'The arteries are cloggin
in motorways and men,
they're deep-fryin floppies
in Silicon Glen,
timor computeris conturbat me.

Soon naebody'll log in
on Scotslit but the profs,
and at the first daimen icker
the thrave'll be flogged off,
timor computeris conturbat me.

Grasp the Internettle
in your ain wee hoose,
and ye'll bide in Bill Gate's kettle
wi a far-frae tim'rous moose,
timor Microsoft conturbat me.

Burns and Hogg and Gibbon
and sad auld mad McGonagall
will be a data ribbon
on some Apple's lap-Macmonocle.
timor computeris conturbat me.

And the Athens of the Forth
whose Socrates was Hume
will be relocated
to a cyber-catacomb.
timor computeris conturbat me.

Dons philosophical
and lecturers on golf
will wax pseudo-topical
on Harris Tweed and Rolf,
post-modernismus conturbat me.

The Auld Alliance means
they'll Derridise their grannies
while central government
replaces them wi jannies
post-modernismus conturbat me.

AI has been found
in a bairn in Achnagash:
just insert potato chips
to avoid computer crash,
timor computeris conturbat me.

While feminists campaign
to disempower the DWAMs,
Wee Bam Bam No-Brain
has jist kicked oot the jams,
timor computeris conturbat me.

With a shit and a click
and a short attention span-ity
the bastard pressed DELETE
on the great works of humanity:
timor computeris conturbat me.'

3

Such a degree of technophobia in
a former ruminant must be symbolic,
I noted; this fixation on high culture
in terms of Scots, a dying leid, confirmed
my diagnosis. Clearly Nessie (as
I'd come to call her) was expressing quite
profound transference with her northern part,
particularly me. Flattered and sad
I pointed out I did not croak allegiance
to Kings Log, Ludd or Shit-Click, handed her
a booklist of more suitable prose models,
bluff urbanites whose drug- and fuck-soaked tales
might touch her slumbering hind-brain. She replied,
'My loins already read them. My head says:
I'm trying to prepare your nation's soul
for its impending literary role.'

Tarzan Visits Highland Region

The crow flies into the Forestry forest, ignoring
the apple core lying on the single track road,
to commune with the spirit of the conifers
about the poor showing by Buckie Thistle
last Saturday, or indeed any Saturday.
The spirit of the conifers, a former seer
whose remains are scattered beneath
the chemists in Beauly, points out
Buckie Thistle did not play last Saturday.
The crow is not convinced there's a distinction.
Meanwhile the apple core, who was a princess
of the Fidach, or Northern Picts, whose bones
lie near a nearby corrugated caravan
(though she is unclear which one), trembles in
her pips with joy, for she alone knows
Tarzan is touring Highland Region.
Tarzan is making slow progress, swinging
on the lianas of larksong left
dangling here and there, because
he has misunderstood the phrase
'Passing Place', and has been attempting
to leave his bowels' vigorous brown signature
in each cupping of gravel.
'Ungowa!' Tarzan says to the midges
but they do not permit him
to ride upon their shoulders.
'Ungowa!' Tarzan says to the sheep
but they do not rescue him from
the morose amorous attentions
of the ghost of the small dog of Hamish MacBeth.
The crow, whose name coincidentally is Cheetah,
remembers an eye it has been meaning to peck
out, and takes its leave of the spirit
of the conifers, who gives it
a pound for a Lottery ticket.
If he wins, he tells the crow, he will buy
a chambered cairn in Tenerife.
The crow considers this unlikely as
it usually drinks the money.

Tarzan approaches the apple core
clutching a bar of McCowans Toffee
given him by a small boy
to whom he had said 'Ungowa!'
though in this instance he was requesting
assistance in ascending into a treehouse.
Tarzan, knowing nothing of her social cachet, fancies
he is in with a chance with the apple core.
The crow passes overhead, heading for
the eyeball. He is flying, as usual,
as the crow flies. Tarzan has
a chat-up line for these occasions
but somehow it has slipped his brain.
Meanwhile in an adjacent field
a little-known prophecy of the former seer
concerning the universal levitation of sheep
is beginning to be fulfilled.

The Gnat Race

Wherever you find a tacit grace
of law and cove, of crop and pace,
you know the cogs of war will place
their excremental colours on its face:
    (the khaki clods are here, are here,
    the khaki clods are here)
the merry lob of uranium shell,
the yomping yobs in Terrier Hotel,
the low-fly jet that ploughs its yell
through barn conversion down to Hell:
catchy as the plaint of the two-headed plaice
is the sub in your net in the Northern Gnat Race.

And hot on the heels of the RAF
come sacred Sue, holistic Geoff,
to sell us smells that quite ineff-
ably cure lumbago if we're deaf:
    (the New Age jerks are here, are here,
    the New Age jerks are here)
their taste for place is so profound
a self-help tape for twenty pound
can rejoin farmers to the ground
where some chief's teeth got left in a mound:
light as the bullet that blows off your face
fall the feet of the the fey in the Northern Gnat Race.

    From Dundrennan to Kirkcudbright
    and from Leuchars to the Neuk,
    from Findhorn through to Lossie
    rest the edges of the Kook
    's Triangle, heather-eaten leavings
    of a ley-like equilateral
    where the fire is always friendly,
    eco-damage just collateral:
    at its UFOmistic centre
    like a walker meshed in midge
    Scotland's jogging on the spot
    known to earth as Bonnybridge.

law: hill.

You can run triangles round us,
use us as a firing range,
compliment our mountains,
find our accent passing strange;
you can purchase books we swear in
find our addicts kind of cool,
for our nation's The Great Gnatsby,
floating face-down in his pool.

How arty to leave the Choke behind
and heave for the neutered North to find
the keeper paint targets on stag and hind,
the cropster collude with the oil-seed grind
of rape and asthmatic villages.
      (the Sunday painters are here, are here,
      the month of Sunday blow-ins)
                                 Look there, between
the Superquarry and the bluey-green
of Loch Algae, beneath the quick-cash screen
of conifer – there's your wild demesne:
escape the judgemental suburban embrace
throw talentless pots in the Northern Gnat Race.

Crystals, pistols, apostles' trout streams,
nets for catching Hopi dreams,
missiles, thistles, fossils who drink malts,
from mystic retreats to armoured assaults,
      (the distance is less than a tare up here,
      the distance is less than a tare)
factors, tractors, reactors, cairns,
from the Bow of Fife to the Howe of the Mearns,
places persist where the Gnat Race can't enter –
as farm-tool museums and deer-life centres:
remember, achieving post-primary place
is just like winning in the Northern Gnat Race.

Mammoth Watch

Dje hear aboot thi latest scam
thae English trehd tae pu?
tae tak oor ain wee mammoth aff –
sic spite wad gar yi grue.

Dje ken oor Shetland mammoth then,
that's knee-heich til a coo,
that huz a coat o orange hair
lyk carrot-coloured spue?

Ut still stravaigs thi Shetland shores
tae sook up strandit whusky
an houks thi mussels aff thi rocks
wi uts weel-adaptit tusky.

Uts eemage is sae picterskew
thi English cam in droves;
thi hauf o whilk wull chess ut roond,
thi ithir hauf jist goaves.

And aa thi while a slee wee scheme
forms in an orra heid
o hoo they cud hauf-inch oor baist –
but whit tae laive insteid?

Therr is a pygmy elephant
that lives aneath thi groond
these wad-be smugglirs saw – an kent
thir cheengelin hud been foond.

Nae maitter that uts tusks werr sma
or that ut micht be cauld
because this pygmy pachyderm
wiz absolutely bald.

---

gar yi grue: make you sick; *stravaigs*: wanders; *houks*: levers; *goaves*: stares
stupidly; *orra*: occasional.

Thae fiendish English lingtowmen
brocht phonies in in cases,
syne wheecht oor Shetland mammoth oot
ablow thi boabbies' fisses.

'Whit wey hae aa oor mammoths tint
thir bonny orange herr?'
'Oh that is just a side-effect
from the wrecking of the Braer.'

'Whit wey can thae wee mammoths no
houk shellfish aff thon rock?'
'Oh that's the VAT on their fuel bills –
they're trembling from shock.'

But syne an eident lass or lad
divined thi awfa truth
an gaithert up thi wrathfu flooer
o Scotia's pugnant youth.

'Wu'll cry wirsels thi Mammoth Waatch
tae guaird agin this crime,
an send thae fause wee elephants
back tae thir Southren clime.'

But when oor canny mammoths hud
arrehvd in sunny Dover,
they set up shoap in ivory
an rowld in gilt-edged clover.

They selt thir ain vom-colourt pelts
back tae thae elephants
wha foond they liked thi Noarth that weel
they werr wearin thermal pants.

An sae thi pair auld Mammoth Waatch
fared ill comparin notes
tae tell thae settlir elephants
frae mammoths truly Scots.

lingtowmen: smugglers; *wheecht*: moved very quickly; *tint*: lost; *syne*: then; *eident*:
keen.

'Oor fauna ut wull atrophy
we still maun dae or deh:
repatriate! repatriate!'
wiz aye thir battle creh.

An sae they kidnapped mammoths fae
thir sonsy Essex bunks
an gote by wey o gratitude
a tawsin fae thir trunks.

They forcit proboscideans
in orange overcoats
by gun-pint doon tae Lerwick pier
and oantae fishin boats.

These refugees focht muckil seas
an sichtit land by morn,
an sae thi whalin elephants
o Norroway werr born;

that tuke thi Pictish sooman hoist
tae grace thir pirate flag,
that flang thir ain tusks fur harpoons
an turnd haill skails tae scag.

EPILOGUE

Gin you shid find ma poem's end
a whit mair soor nor funny
Eh'll scrieve a lauchin close as quick
as you pit up thi money;

ma moral's shairp's a bairnie's hool
whae fae thi breist is weaned:
thae wha ur mellit kulchurs' foe
ur nae wan kulchur's freend.

sonsy: over-comfortable; *tawsin*: beating; *sooman*: swimming; *skails*: schools; *scag*:
fish that has become rotten by exposure to sun or air; *scrieve*: write; *mellit*: mingled,
pluralist.
NOTE: the 'Pictish beast', an mythic figure carved on the symbol stones, has been
described by some commentators as 'the swimming elephant'.

A Difficult Horse

The horse is staring out to sea
from a sloping field not far
out of Aberdeen. I watch it from
the train to Dundee.
It is stationary, staring for
the minute I have it in view.
It is a small brown horse,
possibly even a pony.
The sea is calm. The horse
looks like an old fisherman,
possibly even an old fish.
It's difficult to imagine it ever
moving. It's difficult to know
what it is thinking.
It is a difficult horse.

Cabaret McGonagall

Come aa ye dottilt, brain-deid lunks,
ye hibernatin cyber-punks,
gadget-gadjies, comics-geeks,
guys wi perfick rat's physiques,
fowk wi fuck-aa social skills,
fowk that winnae tak thir pills:
gin ye cannae even pley fuitball
treh thi Cabaret McGonagall.

Thi decor pits a cap oan oorie,
ut's puke-n-flock à la Tandoori;
there's a sculpture made frae canine stools,
there's a robot armadillo drools
when shown a photie o thi Pope,
and a salad spinner cerved fae dope:
gin ye cannae design a piss oan thi wall
treh thi Cabaret McGonagall

We got: Clangers, Blimpers, gowks in mohair jimpers,
Bangers, Whimpers, cats wi stupit simpers –
Ciamar a thu, how are you, and hoozit gaun pal,
welcome to thi Cabaret Guillaume McGonagall.
We got: Dadaists, badass gits, shits wi RADA voices,
Futurists wi sutured wrists and bygets o James Joyce's –
Bienvenue, wha thi fuck are you, let's drink thi nicht away,
come oan yir own, or oan thi phone, or to thi Cabaret.

Come aa ye bards that cannae scan,
fowk too scared tae get a tan,
come aa ye anxious-chicken tykes
wi stabilisers oan yir bikes,
fowk whas mithers waash thir pants,
fowk wha drink deodorants:
fowk that think they caused thi Fall
like thi Cabaret McGonagall.

dottilt: daft, confused; *oorie*: dirty, tasteless; *gowks*: fools; ciamar a thu: how are
you (Gaelic).

Fur aa that's cheesy, static, stale,
this place gaes sae faur aff thi scale
o ony Wigwam Bam-meter
mimesis wad brak thi pentameter;
in oarder tae improve thi species' genes,
ye'll find self-oaperatin guillotines:
bring yir knittin, bring yir shawl
tae thi Cabaret McGonagall.

We got: Berkoffs, jerk-offs, noodles wi nae knickers,
Ubuists, tubes wi zits, poodles dressed as vicars –
Gutenaben Aiberdeen, wilkommen Cumbernauld,
thi dregs o Scoatlan gaither at Chez McGonagall.
We got: mimes in tights, a MacDiarmidite that'iz ainsel contradicts,
kelpies, selkies, grown men that think they're Picts –
Buonaserra Oban and Ola! tae aa Strathspey,
come in disguise jist tae despise thi haill damn Cabaret.

Panic-attack Mac is oor DJ,
thi drugs he tuke werr aa Class A,
sae noo he cannae laive thi bog;
thon ambient soond's him layin a log.
Feelin hungry? sook a plook;
thi son o Sawney Bean's oor cook:
gin consumin humans diz not appal
treh thi Bistro de McGonagall.

Waatch Paranoia Pete pit speed
intil auld Flaubert's parrot's feed,
and noo ut's squaakin oot in leids
naebody kens till uts beak bleeds
and when ut faas richt aff uts perch,
Pete gees himsel a boady search:
thi evidence is there fur all
at thi Cabaret McGonagall.

kelpies: river spirits in the shape of horses; *selkies*: seals which can take on human
form; *leids*: languages.

We got: weirdos, beardos, splutniks, fools,
Culdees, bauldies, Trekkies, ghouls –
Airheids fae thi West Coast, steely knives and all,
welcome to thi Hotel Guillaume McGonagall.
We got: Imagists, bigamists, fowk dug up wi beakers,
lit.mag.eds, shit-thir-beds, and fans o thi New Seekers –
Doric loons wi Bothy tunes that ploo yir wits tae clay;
ut's open mike fur ony shite doon at thi Cabaret.

Alpha males ur no allowed
amang this outré-foutery crowd
tho gin they wear thir alphaboots
there's nane o us can keep thum oot,
and damn-aa wimmen care tae visit,
and nane o thum iver seem tae miss it:
gin you suspeck yir dick's too small
treh thi Cabaret McGonagall.

There's dum-dum boys wi wuiden heids
and Myrna Loy is snuggin stood,
there's wan drunk wearin breeks he's peed –
naw – thon's thi Venerable Bede;
in fack thon auld scribe smells lyk ten o um,
he's no cheenged'iz habit i thi last millenium:
gin thi wits ye werr boarn wi hae stertit tae stall
treh thi Cabaret McGonagall.

We got: Loplops and robocops and Perry Comatose,
Cyclops and ZZ Top and fowk that pick thir nose –
Fare-ye-weel and cheery-bye and bonne nuit tae you all,
thi booncirs think we ought tae leave thi Club McGonagall.
But we got: Moptops and bebop bats and Krapp's Last Tapeworm
          friends,
Swap-Shop vets and neurocrats, but damn-aa sapiens –
Arrevederchi Rothesay, atque vale tae thi Tay,
Eh wish that Eh hud ne'er set eye upon this Cabaret.

Culdees: members of the Columban church; *loons*: young men; *Bothy tunes*: ballads
from the rural North-East; *ploo*: plouh; *foutery*: excessively fussy.

Seagull Blues

Well Eh luked up at grey gulls skriekan
Eh luked doon at peopul speakan
and Eh swerr therr wiz nae diffrence in thi soond
as Eh daunnert thru thi streets
lissnin til thi girns and greets
o thi sowels that flew an waulked thru Dundee Toon.

Huv ye nivir heard ut sedd
that when Alfred Hitchcock dehd
he foond cinematic Heaven kinna dull,
sae he asked thi Filmer o thi Warld
and thi Reel o Life wiz duly birled
but pair Alfie endit up a Dundee gull.

Syne Eve geed'ur man thi appul
a seagull's stapped in ilka thrappul
whas egg wiz seedit in thon appul's core;
when a Dundee boady dehs
anither seagull flehs
crehan oot lyk Poe's auld corbie 'Nevermore!'

Choked oan jute as tho oan feathirs
well ye sune cut oot thi blethirs
sae whit fowk frae here micht sey seems no fur aa
fur ye'll rarely catch thi tune
gin ye've nivir luked abune
and seen thi heavens is thi pit whaur you maun faa.

Thi maas aa swoop lyk freeblawn papirs
and oan lampies cut thir capirs –
cauld yella is thi glinkin o thir beaks –
gin thon's meh granda's ghaist
Eh widna like tae taste
whit he hears ilka time meh grannie speaks.

Well Eh luked up at seagulls speakan
and heard ma bairnie's wurdliss skriekan
and thi tone o canty Casuals' empty keen;
as Eh daunnert Dundee's streets
whaur thi peopul thrang sae fleet
Eh saw thi hungir o thi gull in aa thir een.

The Ballad of Scrapie Powrie

Noo gaither roond baith quine an loon
and a nitherin screed Eh'll read
o hoo auld Scrapie Powrie stole
thi sowels o thi still-waurm deid.

A sandy-heidit lanky lad
that nivir spoke wiz he
that anely by'iz lane wiz glad
i thi hills ahent Dundee.

In seeventeen hunnert and ninety fower
wan dey he went agley
an fur twa-three winter nichts wiz tint
oan the slopes o auld Balgay.

They foond him chitterin in thi haar
an maunderin wi fright
o hoo the Guid Fowk asked 'Wiz he
thi peuchtie o a Pecht?'

Hiz mithir yelpt, hiz faither skelpt
but naither could undae
thae kythes thir loonie thocht he'd seen
i thi weem o auld Balgay.

'A leerie thru thi trees therr wiz
as muckle as thi mune,
a growkin sowff lyk a speildit berg
and an aumrie i thi groon.'

'Thi anely cask that aumeril foond
wiz fuhl o speel-thi-waa,'
hiz faither said – thi boy jist crehd,
'Thon Fairy Court wiz braw!'

quine and loon: young woman and young man; *nitherin screed*: chilling tale; *by'iz lane*: by himself; *ahent*: behind; *agley*-astray; *tint*: lost; *chitterin*: shivering; *haar*: fog from off the sea; *maunderin*: rambling; *peuchtie o a Pecht*: offspring (lit. young coalfish) of a Pict; *skelpt*: slapped; *kythes*: visions; *weem*: cave, womb, stomach; *leerie*: lamp; *growkin sowff*: longing sigh; *speildit*: split; *aumrie*: cupboard cut into a wall; *aumeril*: fool; *speel-thi-waa*: home-made spirit, so bad it made the drinker 'climb the wall'.

'Thir lampies hung in ark-banes therr,
thir clytach ut wiz veive:
thi hauf o aa thir leir an lore
gang thru me lyk a sieve.'

'Thi anely little fowk he met
wiz peerie pintit fungus,'
hiz da explained – thi lad jist maned,
'Thi Deil is among us!'

'Eh saw, Eh saw wan sma wee man
lig doon in a sillery casket,
an shut hiz een, and breath sae slaw –
mair peacefu than disjasket.

'Eh saw thum tak ootfrae'iz heid
a gless o heather yill:
he liggit as he hud been deid,
an therr he's liggin still.

'They helt that unca keltie oot
an losh but ut wiz clear –
Eh kent that gin Eh drank ut doon
Eh'd live twa hunnert year.

'That liquor wiz thon mannie's sowel –
tae keest wad be a sin...'
'That muckle's plain,' hiz pa wiz sayin,
'Thae fairies maun drink gin.'

At that thi elfie-pilkit lad
geed up an shut hiz mou
an nae wurd mair hiz parents heard
o thi wee fowk or thir brew.

By noo ye're mebbe speirin hoo
young Scrapie gote'iz nemm?
Thi thocht o immortality
kept lowein lyk a flemm.

ark-banes: pubic bones; *clytach*: incomprehensible chatter; *veive*: vivid; *leir*: learn-
ing; *peerie*: very small; *lig*: lie; *disjaskit*: exhausted; *heather yill*: liquor brewed
from heather, the secret of making which is supposed to have died out with the
Picts; *keltie*: toast, bumper; *keest*: taste; *elfie-pilkit*: stolen by fairies; *speirin*: en-
quiring; *lowein*: glowing.

Till aff he rade tae Edinbro
a surgeon's trade tae follae
an leirit hoo tae ploutir thru
a boady's ilka hollie.

Thi whilk he did wi sic a virr
– he dagged, he thirlt, he sleeshit –
thi bluid wad slaister Powrie's pow
as tho he had been cleeshit.

An syne'iz glorgy darg wiz din
an syne thir wounds werr cleekit,
and gin hiz patients lived or deed
he luked as he'd been sweekit.

An syne'iz dirty darg wiz din
hiz dirty-drinkan stertit:
aa nicht in howffs aye by'iz lane
wi brains an waur aye clertit.

Nae wunner fowk gote oot iz wey
nor hearkent til'iz havers,
nae wunner he wiz aye thi butt
o ugsome clishmaclavirs.

Therr wiz a donsy servin-lass
wha's nemm wiz Monstrous Meg,
wha Powrie cornert inniz dorts
an hooked oan lyk a cleg.

As fast as she ser'd up'iz yill
he houped ut back lyk waatir,
an blethert oan o ferlies lyk
nae ithir boozir's patter.

'Thi sowel rins doon thi thalamus
lyk seepins in a jakes –
but hoo tae scrape this liquor oot
is geean me thi paiks.'

ploutir: work messily; *hollie*: hollow; *virr*: vigour; *dagged*: stabbed; *thirlt*: pierced; *sleeshit*: slashed; *slaister*: spatter; *pow*: brow; *cleeshit*: whipped; *glorgy*: messy; *darg*: day's work; *cleekit*: hooked together, stitched; *sweekit*: tricked; *clertit*: besmirched; *dirty-drinkan*: drinking by oneself; *ugsome clishmaclavers*: unpleasant rumours; *donsy*: heavy-set, miserable; *dorts*: a low state; *cleg*: horse-fly; *ferlies*: marvels; *jakes*: lavatory; *geean me thi paiks*: causing me a lot of trouble.

'Och, gin uts fusky that yi waant...'
weel-biggit Meg began,
'That's it!' he crehd, 'Thi usquebae
distilled in your brain-pan!'

That nicht – pair Meg – she couldna sleep
withoot a rush-licht's gleid,
an syne she dwaumed that Powrie wiz
ascrapein innur heid.

That morra's morn she heard thi clash
in Candlemaker's Raw:
thi susyliftirs hud been oot –
thi seik glockt innur craw.

That aifternune as she waulked thru
thi feerichin Gressmercat
she heard a heidliss corse wiz foond –
an spued until she jirgit.

That nicht she bent thi landloard's lug
wi sic a fouth o whittirs,
till bluidy Powrie daunnert in –
an syne she hud thi skitters.

Thi landloard peyed'ur little heed
sae til hirsel she muttirt,
'Thi anely wey tae stoap this fiend
is get him mair nor guttirt.'

She powred thi best unwaatird bree
intil a muckle joug,
and ilka time hiz elbuck slacked
she geed ut jist a shoug.

Noo Powrie's jaas werr sune as loose
as Meg's unchancy sphincter,
and owre hur anal trump he yelled,
'Eh am thi grecht restincter!'

fusky, usquebae: whisky; *gleid*: light; *dwaumed*: dreamed; *clash*: conversation;
susylifters: bodysnatchers; *glockt innur craw*: choked up her throat; *feerichin*:
bustling; *jirgit*: made a hoarse noise, dry retched; *a fouth*: a lot; *daunert*: strolled;
skitters: diarrhoea; *unchancy*: unlucky, unpredictable; *restincter*: resurrector.

Nor wan heid birled nor wan lip curled
nor did wan drappie skell,
fur that is hoo a true man treats
a polysyllabell.

Noo Powrie grippit Meggie's airm
tae keep'um staunin straucht:
'Nae frumple sall yir fair fiss feel
gin you wad drink ma draucht!'

Noo you micht think that aa thon drink
micht mak thon haurd tae sey –
meh research shows sic flummry flows
gin ye drink ut ivry dey.

Withoot anither soon syne Meg
linked in and aff they went,
nor in thon howff nor in thon airt
they ivir mair werr kent.

But still an antrin corse waulked aff
fae bane-yairds roond aboot
and wan midnicht a lass wiz seen
wi a dumplin in a cloot.

Nae sae undeemis till ye ken
thi speed that she wiz fuddin,
or jidge that fae thi trail o dreeps
thon wiz a bluidy pudden.

Nae wurd wiz heard o Powrie nor
Miss Feery-o-thi-feet,
till twa loons foond an aumrie cut
intil King Arthur's Seat.

Thi twa-fut doors werr medd o slate
they flang intil a linn;
inside werr seeventeen wee kists
fyke-fackit up wi tin.

birled: whirled round; skell: spill; frumple: wrinkle; flummry: flattery; airt: part;
antrin: occasional; cloot: cloth; undeemis: unusual; fuddin: running swiftly like a
startled rabbit; Feery-o-thi-feet: a swift runner; linn: stream; kists: chests; fyke-
fackit: fussily decorated.

Within aa these fir-feckits werr
wee shroodit wuiden lodgirs –
thi whilk we'd find a fickler but
thae lads jist pleyed at sodgers.

Sae hauf this resurrectit troop
then met a second daith
afore thi laddies' maws werr telt
wha telt men o thi claith.

These kent this wiz thi Deevil's wark
withoot thi need tae see ut
thi wey some fowk laith Crappit Heids
withoot thi need tae pree ut.

An sae a guid auld-farrant hunt
fur witches then begood,
and by hauf-fowre thon sel-same dey
they'd plucked oot quite a brood.

They scranched a foot in ilka Boot
thi meenisters could borrae,
but tho thi skreiks went oan fur weeks
they sune began tae worry.

Fur tho thi witches aa confessed
– fur witches like tae plaise –
nae story mentioned wuiden men
dressed in thir funeral claes.

They stagged thum fuhl o witchin-peens,
they dooked thum in a loch,
but o thi seeventeen wee men
they heardna eech nor och.

And sae thi maitter wad hae endit
wi weel-attendit burnins
till a drucken kiltie stoappit Meg
and oaffert hur'iz earnins.

fir-feckit: pine-jacket, euphemism for a coffin; *fickler*: puzzler; *Crappit Heids*: stuffed
heads of haddock; *pree*: taste; *begood*: began; *scranched*: crushed; *Boot*: instrument
of torture which broke the bones of the foot and shin; *stagged*: stabbed; *dooked*:
dipped; *eech nor och*: not the smallest sound; *kiltie*: member of a Highland regi-
ment.

'But Ah maun tak this panyell hame
and gee ma man hiz hough.'
'Fae hough tae houghmagandie, lass,
thi distance is a troch.'

He trehd tae tak'ur basket, sayin,
'Eh'll pey fur this and aa,'
whan fae this fouterie strachil syne
a severt heid did faa.

Ut skitit aff doon Cockburn Street
an yi could hae cut thi quiet,
till thi sodger piped up, 'Fegs, yir man
is oan an unca diet.'

Weel they haaled hir up afore thi kirk
and they brent hir beam an broo
but nary a wurd wad Meggie speak
till they trehd thi auld thumbscrew.

Ah've burnt morel that mony times
oan stoves Ah feel nae smert,
but gin ye pirl thon screw aince mair
ma mooth'll brak ma hert.'

As sune as baith hir thoombs werr girstle
an Powrie wiz arrestit,
they foond hiz chaumirs fu o skulls
aa o thir harns divestit.

But waur – they foond thi jaaboax fu
o minds aa in a mammock,
wi a wuid man in't – but waur by faur,
they foond they'd shared a hammock.

Tae poond a boady's brenns tae jeel
and flocht a doll therein –
that's bad, but sex unsanctifehd –
that is a mortal sin.

---

panyell: basket; *hough*: brawn; *houghmagandie*: sexual intercourse; *troch*: a small
thing, a bargain; *fouterie strachil*: fumbling struggle; *brent*: burnt; *pirl*: turn; *harns*:
brains; *jaaboax*: sink; *mammock*: mush.

Auld Scrapie Powrie rantit lood
o hoo he helt thi pooer
tae raise thi deid oan Jupiter
gin he didna miss thi 'oor.

'Ye've killt thum twice, ye gomerils,
ye feechy preachin ghouls:
Eh'd resurrect by science whaur
ye're murderin thir sowels!'

And here he luked at Monstrous Meg
and here she gan tae greet,
'Thi seepins that we baith hae shared –
tae sin thus wiz sae sweet.'

They tuke them up oan Arthur's Seat
whaur thi brands werr stookit neat,
but as sune as they wad licht thi pyres
thi weather turnit weet.

And fur a week this witchcraft warked
and renn upset thi pley
until thi sun rose bricht an waurm
upon a Munondey.

Whan thi kail-bell rang they lit thi wuid
and Powrie geed a hoast,
but syne, afore thi bleeze could ganch
they baith geed up thi ghost.

Thi meenisters hud hoped fur mair,
thi crood wiz black affrontit;
insteed o screels an sorry screeds
thi pair hud scarcely gruntit.

Sae whan thi tinkle-sweetie rang
and aa wiz banes an ricks
jist wan auld tinkie steyed tae roast
hiz tatties in thi sticks.

---

gomerils: imbeciles; *feechy*: filthy; *kail-bell*: dinner-bell; *hoast*: cough; *bleeze*: blaze; *ganch*: bite, take hold; *screels*: yells; *tinkle-sweetie*: bell rung around 8 p.m., when shops were closed; *ricks*: columns of smoke, remains of a fire.

Nae gadgie's ivir heard hiz tale
apairt frae thi Powrie clan,
fur'iz great-grandochtir came an telt
thi hail o't tae meh great-gran.

Thi waurmth, he said, hud made him bide
lang eftir daurkniss fell;
thi gleid wiz bricht eneuch tae read
– no that he could himsel.

Thi mune wiz ridan heich an pale,
thi ling wiz dreh an saft;
he wiz sittan happy doavrin whan
he heard a snappin chaft.

Thi soond came frae thi faurest pyre
whaur Powrie hud been burned;
thi answer came sae close he thankt
thi Loard'iz heid wiz turned.

Thi twa skulls clackt lyk castanets,
thi tinker he did freeze;
fur he thocht he heard twa dreh wee groans
come flochtin in thi breeze.

Thi wan said 'Sall they nivir cam?'
thi tither answert 'Wait:
therr's still a witness oan thi hill
wha hiz a hert tae beat.'

Thi tinker's weem wiz speelin up
hiz thrapple lyk a squirrel,
thi tinker's bluid wiz stoundin thru
hiz veens wi a hirdum-dirl.

But syne anither twa wee stevins
flew lichtly thru thi whins:
'Sall we laive'iz harns inside'iz heid
upo thi heckle-pins?'

gadgie: non-gypsy; ling: heather; doavrin: half-sleeping; chaft: jaw; thrapple: throat;
stoundin: pounding; hirdum-dirl: a loud pounding beat; stevins: voices; heckle-pins:
a state of great uncertainty.

'Or sall we howk'um oot'iz neb
thi wey thi Egyptians did?'
And he kent thi Little Fowk hud come
upon him in a whid.

Ae mazzard askit, 'Wha ur these
wha end oor dowie wait?'
Thi tither snapped, 'Eh carena wha
as lang's they're nae too late.'

At this wan daffin bird-like voice
said, 'See this scuitifu?
Hoo wad he like ut gin Eh kissed
hiz wumman's lipless mou?'

'A limbless man leirs patience,' lauched
thi ithir elf wi relish.
'Sir Scoup, meet Shabby Harlicks and
hiz guid freend Jolly Welsh.'

'He fain wad be a sclushach's fere,'
said Shabby, 'sall we hurry?
An syne we can come back and scare
thi sowel ootfrae this scoury.'

Thi chitterin tinkie shut hiz een
an crullit in a baa:
tae see thi Wee Fowk or be touched –
that widna dae ava.

'Ye've scomfished him,' said wan, and syne,
sae near he felt uts spittle,
thi ither speerit speirit, 'Sall
Eh gee wir man a kittle?'

'Thi 'oor, thi 'oor!' ae skull burst oot,
and aa uts teeth did claik;
thi tither said mair doucely, 'Sirs,
we fain wad mak oor wake.'

---

whid: an instant; *mazzard*: skull; *dowie*: mournful; *scuitifu*: the contents of a scoop-
shaped drinking cup; *scoup*: skull; *sclushach*: a crab after it has cast its shell, a
slovenly woman; *fere*: companion; *scoury*: disreputable type; *crullit*: shrank in on
oneself; *ava*: at all; *scomfished*: discomfited; *kittle*: tickle; *doucely*: gently.

'Dje hear thon fliskmahago plead?
But since ye ask sae nice
We'll hae ye baith oan Jupiter
in somethin lyk a trice.'

'Oan Jupiter or in this hill
or somewhaur else insteid,
fur ilka grave's a vehicle
unto a daithliss heid.'

'Ah Powrie, whaur's yir science noo,
and whaur's yir luvir's breist?
Therr is nae difference tae thi sowel
tween this warld and thi neist.'

'But since that's hoo yir mind hiz set,
that's hoo ye sall survive,
and ye sall meet yir Meggie there,
baith fleeshless but alive.'

Wi that therr wiz a michty lowe
that aa at Wallce went cauld
and thi tinker foond hiz tatties charred
an'iz heid completely bauld.

In case ma grecht-grandmithir thocht
hir story wisna true,
thi lassie tuke hir heidscarf aff
hir herrliss pate and broo.

Syne trehd tae sell'ur twa auld skulls
that smelt lyk twa new kippers –
meh grecht-granminnie chessed hir aff
by peltin'ur wi'ur slippers.

But thae twa skulls helt pride o place
upo hir mantelpiece
lyk wallie-dugs – or mair lyk bools,
since she geed'um elby-grease.

fliskmahago: loose woman; *neist*: next.

An noo an then at unca 'oors
or sae meh faither claims
yi heard a faur-by murmellan
o near-forgettlet nemms.

Sae pair auld Powrie micht be richt
as thocht thon Disney geezir;
sae get yir ain deid heid cut aff,
an stap ut in a freezir.

faur-by: distant; *stap*: stuff.

Ballad of the Ship Inn

Oot past Bell Rock
in thi deep
sailors' een
in saalty sleep,

waves ur toarn up
by thi beach,
gless o whusky
in meh reach,

pints o heavy
haud the mune –
's a pickilt ingin
fetch a spune,

gin Eh et ut
braith wad hum
o sichtliss een
in ocean's wumb.

ingin: onion.

Byculture

All scripts were music to us
who could not read, nor break
the secrecy of instruments;

all keyboards dummy, all codes
mute barriers, so beautiful
we camped outside your cities

for centuries, besieging you
and dissecting those who issued
forth for traces of schematics.

We mimicked what we could
eavesdrop, no mynah more
uncomprehending, no hound

more lovestruck. We followed
your engines through the ruins
of our mothers' households,

across the tufa that had been
our fathers' fields until
every nuance could be aped.

By then the last of you had
confessed the key to all
you sang and said was long

lost, and left us for silence.

EAST OF AUDEN

'More specifically of the North East, the working class
culture is strongly male-orientated, macho you might
say. In terms of this male chauvinism, then, poetry is
an activity that only wimps would practice (or boys who
were 'girl's blouses' as my aunt would say), and Geordie
men don't want to see themselves as wimps. Against
this general background it's surprising that any poetry
has come out of the region since the Second World War.
Dut It has.'

GEORGE CHARLTON

'Mrs Carritt, my tea tastes like tepid piss.'

W.H. AUDEN

Road Movie

> *'As a boy, I often used to ask myself if there really
> was a God who saw everything. And how he man-
> aged not to forget any of it: the motion of the clouds
> in the sky, every individual's gestures and footsteps,
> the dreams...I said to myself that while it was im-
> possible to imagine such a memory existing, it was
> even sadder and more desolating to think that it
> didn't and everything was forgotten. This childish
> panic still upsets me. The story of all phenomena
> would be infinitely great, the story of all surviving
> images infinitesimally small.'*

> WIM WENDERS: 'A history of imaginary films',
> from *The Logic of Images*

1

I'm trying to remember that drive
from Otterburn to Carter Bar
six years ago, when we married
each other repeatedly, making up
ceremonies as we drove, picking
locations out of memories or maps
or books, but it's like searching
a video of film-fragments for
one scene, probably recorded over.
The road spins everything past
into peripherality, like brand
placements in movies; only driving
it again reveals the names:
Elishaw, Redesdale, Catcleugh.
Only God was filming us then,
for all the focus of our loving
each other, that makes everything
into story, only God recorded how
what we saw and said was forced
by passion into narrative.

I'm thinking: the week before
the beginning of the world,
what did God do? Some portion must
have driven round Northumbria as
He knew it would become, in His
Model Alpha and Omega, each
angel contracted to a thin
white stripe with one cat's eye
and lying in a line upon the void.
Did He speed down empty roads
from Newcastle to Berwick,
then, without changing gear,
from Amble to Rothbury, over
and over, drawing a cross across
the county absent-mindedly? I'd
have to ask an angel. Did
Satan ask, 'Where could Your mind be,
O Lord, when You are being absent-
minded?' and God reply, 'It is
going to and fro upon the A1,
and driving up and down on it...'?

He must already have been listening
outside time as we are outside
a film, to wheels crunch on gravel,
that idiolect of John Macadam's,
distinctive as the 's's of Connery.
We were already his memories
as we drove, of the small actions
we were only then performing
for the first and liberating time.

2

The feeling while driving alone at night that the car is full of spirits, picked up like burrs from the places driven through. Who would star in your movie but these silent companions, wingless angels? Some kind of bonding must be occurring between these unseen passengers and your unspeaking role. During the day it's fainter, like memories of films seen as a child, like films seen in a previous life. Ghosts of actors crowd your car, travelling aimlessly between morning reruns, no one actually watching, just the un-focussed eye of the unemployed, a housewife, a worker-from-home eating lunch. The blind stroking transferrence to video tape.

So it's night, no one's dead yet, you play the rational sentry resist-ing the cry of 'Who sits there?' But back the daft, betraying answers creep from the back of your head. I, Barbara Stanwyck, sitting in a rickshaw in the middle of a riot. I, Katharine Hepburn, with a leopard in the back. I, Bette Davis, in the cholera cart. I, Grace Kelly, with a cold buffet of chicken legs and breasts and beer. I, Cary Grant, injected with youth serum mixed by a monkey. I, Jimmy Stewart, parking on the ridiculous hills of San Francisco. I, Rod Steiger, pointing a gun at Brando. I, Jimmy Dean, about to play the Chicken Run.

So many weird passwords you laugh, but you're still scared to switch the radio on in case it starts giving birth to stars, angrily grunting out slick platinum pentangles through the tear in the speaker.

3

I'm driving from Tynemouth to
a rented flat in Amble, thinking
the chimneys of Blyth look like
they're plugged into a sky full
of dissipating saltires, its
aeroplane memoires. I'm thinking
of that first time we drove
to Edinburgh together, not lovers
yet, Kelleher in the back. I'd like
to write down that I'm remembering,
but no notes if you're driving;
the flow makes you mute,
like sitting in God's cinema.

I try that photograph you took
as a mnemonic, like a still
from the film only angels watch,
Warholian, the pure unfolding
of days, from each person's POV.
I'm halfway up a lamppost in
Newbiggin, bare-footed, climbing
into the sky up its rope trick
of light, unaware that my world
has just stopped floating; no
more drinking like a Daoist.
The next reel was sex comedy;
I would have to be seduced
as usual, to stop me drifting
further upwards, brushing
against their frozen-lashed lens.
After the lamppost scene you drove
us to Druridge Bay, we all ran
from the tawny fringe of dunes
into the cold August sea.
I can't remember who kept their
pants on: have to ask an angel.

We remade that movie when
we married ourselves, creeping into
the Saxon crypt at Ripon Cathedral,
improvising our promises in
its old buried dark, before
the lights burst in on us for
the day's first tourists. Then
back to the bay, no pants at all,
lots of photos of wet hair, champagne,
genitalia sherberted with sand, same
sound-track of Lou Reed to take
us north to Gigha and Loch Tay.

4

'It is not really possible for us to say what angels look like to other angels.'
EILEEN ELIAS FREEMAN, quoted in
Scotland on Sunday, 10 July 1994

The angel of internal combustion looks like
a nodding dog the size of Iceland.
The angel of Hillman Minxes
looks like Thunderbird Two.
The angel of spark plugs looks like a spark plug.

Each night all the angels cram into
a pet shop in Berwick
and weep gently into chamois leathers.

The angel of global warming looks like
Michael Caine in *Get Carter*.
The angel of cigarette lighters
looks like a parrot.
The angel of Saabs looks like a sun-dried tomato.

Each night all the angels gather in
the Bar of Wingless Compassion
and discuss rust. On Fridays it's WD-40.

The angel of the A1 looks like
a large book each page of which
is made of crushed crashed cars.
His wings are the covers
each feather of which is a name.

Each night all the angels drive around
a crazy golf course in Morpeth
and sing crankshaft shanties.

The angel of taxi drivers is invisible
but smells of mince.
The angel of parrots looks like a cigarette lighter.
The angel of Ford Capris
looks like two blue furry dice.

Each night all the angels gather in
the Bar of the Soft-boiled Halo
and consume a liquor made from antifreeze.

The angel of the movies is dreaming of his unshot children; of unmade genres like the Borderers, tales of midge-bitten cattle men, rustlers and renegades in the Debatable Lands between England and Scotland in the fifteenth and sixteenth centuries. Men whose quick-drawing skill with the flintlock was ahistoric but legendary, men whose Samurai-like code of honour required them to live and die by the claymore. Women as untamed as the Northumbrian hills, but not as broad, as wild as the Scottish wildcat, as passionate as the Irish actresses who would usually get the parts.

The angel dreams of how Hollywood could have loved the legendary showdown between the Douglases and the Percies in *Gunfight at Otterburn Paddock*; the classic triumph of the wee antiques dealer in *MacShane*; the elegiac portrait of the auld reivers in *She Wore a Tartan Ribbon*; the box-office smash combination of Paul Newcastle and Robert Redeswire in *Kinmont Willie and the Melrose Kid*. The very names conjure up a virtual era of movie magic: imagine the young Elizabeth Taylor's terrible Scottish accent in *Lassie Crosses the Border*; or *The Magnificent Borderers*, the only film in which Orson Welles could have directed Yul Brynner; John Ford's late masterpiece *The Quiet Borderer*; and that iconoclastic sixties road movie, *Borderers on Bikes*. So resonant might the theme have been that even Europeans could have responded: who can remember the Hungarians' Goulash Borderers trilogy: *For a Fistful of Thistles, For a Few Thistles Mair*, and *The Good, the Bad, and the Northumbrian*? The genre could even have adapted itself to crossovers: musicals like *Reivin in the Rain*, and of course, horror (how many would have shrieked, possibly with laughter, at Vincent Price's performance in *The Well of the Wife of Usher*?)

The angel (who resembles an old-fashioned projectionist's room, full of stacks of film canisters, curling posters of stars and the giant food-mixer of the camera) considers famous names never associated with the Borderers. Ulverston alumnus Stan Laurel, who, after the tragically premature death of his comedy partner, could have directed the magical *Wizard of Ercildoune*, with its haunting theme tune 'Somewhere Over the Border'. Claude Raines, whose amoral Gilbert de Umfraville could have uttered the immortal line, 'Round up the usual Borderers.' Alexander MacKendrick, whose disastrous Hollywood career might have been turned around by the hilarious *Mint Cake Galore*. Bill Forsyth, who might have revitalised a declining form with his painstakingly-researched, Oscar-winning epic,

Dances with Capercaillies. And what about Bill Douglas's existential wildlife tragedy, *Waiting for the Third Corbie*, in which all the dialogue is between two ravens sitting smoking on the corpse of a knight (academy awards could have gone to Billy Connolly and – posthumously – Mark McManus for their voice-overs)?

Stars of the Border screen flicker across the editing suite of his imagination: silent unpredictable Kirk Whelpington, pretty songbird Tillie Throckley, laconic dependable Long Framlington, garrulous sidekick Elishaw Whitters, and the musical reiver himself, Rob Roy Rogers. Ah, for the long-ago Saturday mornings that never happened, when kids would run to see the non-existant Borderers; the angel of the movies wakes up in a melancholy mood, moisture filling his celluloid eyes.

6 *(an epithalamion of wings)*

In Ripon, Melrose, Gigha, by Loch Tay,
our wedding bed was spread across
two countries and four days.
One angel's voice
still says

this: 'Feir
God. Fle from Sin.
Mak for the Life Ever-
lesting to the End.' His words carved in
a Borders doorframe, ordering, unclear.

7

*'Any era, from the ancient world of the Nile to the Victorian age,
can be fascinating when you add the vampire myth.'*

VAMPIRE: THE MASQUERADE
(a role-playing manual)

The road keeps becoming
a journey between angels,
beginning with the red cliff jaw
of Burghead's Pictish variety,
which I had just made up
before we flitted south;
his brethren do four-winged
acrobatics up the side
of Sueno's stone at Forres.
Here he was swilling the firth
for distillations of bottle-
house song tasting for traces
of glossolalia, while I had to chase
your Prozac-high brother,
driving a hired van full
of our domestic essentials,
a few shelves of library
and boxes gilled with papers
like square fungi, almost
into the fingerless glider arms
of the future angel of Gateshead.

Dad took over at Dundee, did
the Coldstream road to Central
Station in three hours, knowing
our Dean Moriarty impersonator,
our Fitzcarraldo of serotonin in
the transit ark, could be counted on
to park outside the County Hotel
in a trust-free zone called
Saturday night in Newcastle,
and go, guilt and padlock free,
to his prepaid Geordie bed.

All roads are low by night,
weariness expressing itself in
the sense of pushing against
companies of the dead, filing

113

home from Flodden, never
arriving. The verges are bled
to black and white, crowded
with rabbit extras; they eat,
casual as flaneurs at cafés
at a Parisian location, turn
the movie into a drama of
the Occupation, the ghosts
becoming Nazi troops. Grey trees
reiterate the Arc de Triomphe
until the road straightens,
becomes pilum-sure and Roman.
The car still seems to drive
through a wash of marching;
the Ninth legion, surely,
Mithra-worshipping, lost.
The mind is channel-hopping,
the driving is a drift toward
sleep, the giant owls of
occasional headlights scarcely
rouse us as we speed past Morpeth.

Amazingly we beat him, arriving first
and pacing the empty streets,
avoiding bucktoothed drunks
I think: now's the time to film,
in the Georgian silence of
the Lit & Phil, of Grey Street's
derelict corner; something
should appear, a dray, the hooves
of the horses muffled, pushed
by a whole pack of Nosferatus,
containing giant fossils,
trilobites and coelocanths,
ammonites the size of fridges,
and pull up outside the hotel.
One will hand me a card like they filled
the screen with in the silents.
It will say: 'Here's your luggage.'

8

Driving to Blyth in the morning induces a pleasurable mixture of anxieties. First there are instructions to be followed, which turns driving into an ordeal like assembling an elephant from a kit without knowing what an elephant is whilst suffering from elephantiasis. As it is, the instructions are coherent, and you only make one mistake, which makes you late.

Second there is the weather. This morning is both very misty and very bright. This is such an unusual combination it reminds you of a train trip down the east coast in which you couldn't see the sea. You could see the beach and the horizon, but everything in between was low-lying dazzling mist. It looked as though the North Sea had been replaced by steam. Possibly even turned to steam by strategically placed submarines set to boil over. Perhaps troops were advancing even then through the desert foothills of the Dogger Bank, filling their packs with suffocated fish found flapping in their path.

But you must concentrate; the actual moment at which you will become officially late is fast approaching, and you still have not found the road to Blyth. You float around mini-roundabout after mini-roundabout, at which the air is so full of mist that has been so filled with light that you cannot read the exit signs, so you must go round them one more time before floating off down a possible route to Blyth.

At these moments you feel you could be abducted by aliens like on the video you were watching the previous night. Would you even know? Perhaps you have already been abducted and are now carrying repressed and traumatic memories. At these moments you feel the air is full of the wings of seraphim beating rolling clouds of mist upon you and misleading you in your quest. You realise that the actual moment you should have arrived is upon you and you still have not found the road to Blyth. A sense of great peace and freedom from the values and constraints of your workaday life descends upon you.

Touching Lot's Wife

It's that God again; the sort of deity
who doesn't need to use our viruses,
our gases or our bombs, when He feels
like searing out some thousands of us.
Can't you recognise His handwriting in
that angular strafe of lightning? Any
graphologist would say: 'Dominating, but
creative.' That Geordie mother is
impersonating him right now, stabbing at
the little vertical loaf that was Lot's wife,
showing to her daughters how
this whole world billows at Jahweh's whorl.
I shudder too, still believing it's not nice
to touch art, wondering: would that finger,
placed on her children's tongues, taste
of more than her own salt? For this
vast canvas has that old God's finger-
print all over it, stirring the too-hot
porridge that was Sodom – or Gomorrah,
she's not saying. Maybe it's too near to home
to ask why this great foundry of souls
was lit and then put out, as if
the generations were a flicking switch:
ON the keyboard kids, OFF the coal-caked miners.
It looks like a fleet of dreadnoughts, gone
down burning in some massive Corryvreckan.
The father stands to one side, slightly
bored by all this dried-up daubing,
like squares of camouflage
between us and the work-starved streets,
maybe abashed by Lot's daughters being
first offered up to would-be angel-rapers
then lying with Lot anyway, drunken in the fells,
to give life to Moab and Ben-ammi. Perhaps
one daughter no longer equals one angel,
and no one's seed now seems to need such
preserving. Is he too noting the hot
invisible spirtle this kind of God employs
for destroying His bowl of bad men?

116

The painting has stopped quivering.
The nuclear unit leaves, leaving me
to see something further, not Lot's wife as
the original fag-hag, caught in a blash
of oceanic sperm, nor the Jackson Pollock that
John Martin made of his sky, but
a single fingerprint, filling the frame,
composed of myriads of salty fingertips:
a whole city pointing, identifying by
their uncowed need to touch, their own refusal
to dodge or budge or be extinguished.

Sticking the Leaves Back On

They should still be here, a slice
of green gone orange through
the giant Dan Dare visor of
our third-floor thirties flat window,
as they were when we arrived, before
the shipyard had been officially closed.

But I forgot to note their off broccoli tone
through the glass's frigidaire effect
before the season changed in one night
of soot blown into our grate
embossed ATOM as though anticipating
its conversion to plutonium central heating
in the perfect tupperware future
I find myself now occupying.

No helicars descended through
the schizoid wrought-iron work
of bare black branches, but
the chainsaws impersonated those
ghosts of the post-war's future as
men removed dead trees in
great gear-like rounds. I held my daughter
to the glass supposedly showing her
that anomaly: a craneless view in Newcastle,
but she slapped the pane with her seven month
spitty palms and watched instead
the hard-hatted surgeons nearly
but never quite saw through
the branches they were sitting on.

Then I saw, between my visits to
the opera, the galleries, all
the rituals of arrival in
the culture of a new city,
that I would have to creep out in a darkness
and glue the moth-brown leaves back on
these lifeless surviving sticks:
or what else would there be
for my daughter to grow up seeing?

Garibaldi's Head

*'Þa læg se græge wulf þe bewiste þæt heafod, and mid his twam
fotum hæfde þaet hæfod beclypped, grædig and hungrig, and for
or Gode ne dorste þæs heafdes abyrian, [ac] heold hit wið deor.'*
ÆLFRIC's *Life of St Edmund*

Kick it down the hill, you blue-brained kids,
bury it deep in the nearest to woods
    that Blaydon's got.
Thank your longest straw there's not
a red-shirt she-wolf hereabout
to dig the head of the patriot up,
put her paw upon it, and treat it like her pup.

Gather up the flies from his trunk of liberty,
mash them into biscuit mix and nibble for your tea
    on the very idea
of beatifying radicals in stone.
Statues should be admirals, aristocrats, Homerical;
a foreign common hero is just tastelessly chimerical.
Bury deep the thousand-headed mob-dog's bone.

But Garibaldi's head will not be good, stay hidden;
though you dunk it into duck-pond,
though you muddle it with midden,
it still serenades the severed moon, a hopeful sound;
    although you've tried
stuffing up your doctrines with bog rhetoric and pride,
society's the pitch you can't punt the head outside

of. Coffin up his torso in an estuarial pile,
blue-plaque his genteel Tynemouth lodgings,
wear your retriever's newsprint smile,
explain he was a royalist and full of moral fudgings,
    clench your fist:
remember how King Edmund's corpse united with his head;
God darned his throat together left a single scarlet thread.

That's the common hue that still repairs the trousers
on faith's arse, grind down your teeth with biting
as you will, but you're ageing Tory towsers
and you'll never pass for vikings
            now, still less sharks.
Having lied through plenty daylights you can lie there in the dark
and listen through the illness for the three sharp barks
you know, despite the knowledge that your noodle's growing mouldy,
mean 'Bring me the head of Guiseppe Garibaldi!'

'In 1868, a statue of Garibaldi was erected on Summerhouse Hill. The statue was
slightly larger than life size, and showed Garibaldi, holding the telescope and wear-
ing the sword with which he'd been presented in 1854, looking eastward down the
Tyne. The statue was sculpted by George Burn of Newcastle.

About 1900 the statue was toppled from its plinth and rolled, broken, down the
hill. Due to this the head, exhibited here, shows signs of damage. It was found in a
builder's yard in Blaydon in 1941, and donated to the library in 1977.'

– *Inscription in Blaydon Library*

Hard Hat Heaven

'Art equals the death of industry,' squeals
the nearest melancholy mouth of the six
six-foot Sci-fi ventilator caps turning
on top of the Baltic Flour Mills building
like Newcastle's depleted unseen muses in
the bright recorded air of a radio programme.
We're here because the Mills are turning
slowly into a gallery, grant by Millennial
grant; they're planning to gralloch it, leaving
two walls like a hollowed sandwich, to be filled
with glass and a pickle of installations.
We're cosying a microphone from the gusts
with our coat-flaps like the chick-protecting
kittiwakes who've colonised this brick cliff,
our hard hats yellow as the breakfast eggs
they'll work up here when the roof's a café.
We're trying not to shout and gazing down
on egg-white washy river-ideograms
reflected off the latest glass-faced blocks.
We know that what they say is 'unship', 'uncoal',
but try to praise the it-iness of cities
instead, the bits we can't quite see from up
here: how the shopfront lettering of 'DOG
LEAPANTIQUES' makes new space, scored with traces
of springing hounds. Or the formula 'DOM=ALE'
sketched on Clayton Road's railway bridge
as though this breakthrough would be lost
if not noted immediately. Or the dogfish with its
nose bitten off in Tynemouth's *Sealife Centre*;
or that UBU stands for 'Universal Bedding
and Upholstery' on West Chirton Industrial Estate
(Jarry did say 'Life is fiction'); or
the obese Vikings whose statues stand
in Jarrow, considering a betting shop; or
that the buses say 'Wear Buses' on their noses.
These things make up our daily alphabet;
they are our scattered necessary urban grain.
So who's missing from the muses? Simple,
the relevant ones: all history, all tragedy, any

whiff of epic's yeast the revolt of industry held,
has all been wiped in favour of a gallery.
Who's left? a disquietingly irrelevant sextet:
Urania, muse of astronomic cost; Thalia,
muse of the pastoral, or here, of Byker Farm
(let them drink goats' milk); Polyhymnia and
Terpsichore – now we know we're in the reign
of Ming the Meaningless, Emperor of Mime
and Extemporary Prance. Did Erato wail?
But who needs melody while we have Jimmy Nail?
And lastly lies Euterpe, on her lyric side,
Dale Arden of the Tyne, stunned by Ming's Ray
of Mediocrity. We flail round for a Gordon,
a flash of Socialist Realism *ex machina galactica*
or just a stiff anaesthetising gin,
but all we see's that 'LEE BOY WAS HERE' before us.
Entering through the condemned interior,
the hundred-teated Diana of grain, whose robes are
monastral green and fifties industrial custard,
he would have toed over the kittiwakes' library
of two abandoned books, then climbed the cold
egg-strewn stairs, maybe reading from
*Safety Precautions for Employees Entering Grain
or Product Basins*: '2. A code of audible
emergency signals shall be arranged between
the man in the bosun's chair or cage
and the responsible person at the top of the bin...'.
Then, emerging onto the roof, meditatively
spraying the bricks, did Lee Boy look
upriver at the lovely bridgework, and down
at the piss-poor dentistry done now
on shipyard and empty site? Probably not.
(This is not yet the place for Howson's *Noble Dosser*:
Lee no doubt lacks the musculature to hulk.)
Did he wonder when that responsible person first
went deaf to the ventilation system's drone,
or where they went to? Probably knew the pub.
That could mean it's left to me to be
unable to stop imagining that previous man,
still in the bosun's chair, but stranded,
swinging between the two remaining walls
as though between the hulls of two ships,

both passing him by and between them as
they steadily go. That sort of thing's my job.
That and noting nobody but Lee Boy would
record himself, whereas I could swear, mealie-
mouth-parts audible to the small all
which listens to that sort of station, that art
can only satisfy a city's palate, and
galleries are not the issue; something else
is showing here that none of us will stomach.

Bede's World

On the metro to the monastery I ping out
a filling whilst picking my teeth with a pen top,
pop it back into place and bite down hard.
It stays. I get off at Bede Station and make
pilgrimage through industrial estate;
by dual carriageway I walk me along.

Soon there is no pavement, just a track
around the timber yard and over a weak bridge:
'BUY AN OUNCE AND YOU'LL BE STONED ALL DAY'
grey spraypaint on its blue metal side advises.
Instead I visit Bede's World.

                  A longhair,
more gonk than monk, meditates with plastic bag
in the grounds of St Paul's, while I pass
an Asian couple in matching sky-blue grinding
gently together in the lane by the Don
where the kitchen garden would have sloped.

I have gone the long way round to get in
to the eighth century it seems, looking back
over the wall at cranes and drums and half-
empty car-parks hemmed in by a fence of pylons
and the lack of ships in Tyne Port.

The kids, who may not be alright, have kicked
in the floodlights, taking out portions
of fourteenth century with them. I check out
the interior for lumps of vinescrolling
and the Jarrow lectures: 'The Codex Amiatinus
and the Byzantine element in the Northumbrian
Renaissance', 'Early Christianity in Pictland'.

The women minding the church's shop have
an engrossing rosary of others' ailments
to recite, filling the site with a locality
its surroundings continue to deny.

The museum most of all – with its salmon-
pastel round of brick and paddle-pool blue
of fountain, more atrium than cloister,
more Roman than Catholic – is not here.

Inside you pick up telephones to hear
the Gododdin spoken in Old Welsh,
like cricket results or the weather,
and think how fleetingly theme parks catch
the attention of their visitors, like

a swallow flying into a hospital ward,
full of a terror shared by those in every bed,
battering itself off too much glass before
finding a way back out into the world.

Outside, withies and wattles prevail,
old breeds of hog and sheep and bull
from Ronaldsay and other outer zones
are clustered in the dark age hollow,
emmer, spelt and einkorn grow together in
the one authentic field, while a timber hall
and grubenhaus are being copied from
genuine remains.

                Only this incompletion
seems real: the workmen's radio tuned in
to a golden hour as None approaches is
as dependable as Bede's voice singing
'Ter hora trina uoluitur'; the photocopied
labels on the fences as trustworthy as
the copy of his *Historia* displayed
indoors as a superb example of Insular
miniscule script.

                Only our discrepancies
are real here; our marches in the face
of parliament, our writings in despite
of the vikings, even our theme parks
in the midst of recession, are bits
picked out from the sad mixture flowing
between black mud banks and made our own.

Theory and Function of Invisibility

I want to be Columbo with no murders to solve,
I want to be Columbus in a world
with no more Americas, no Indies,
I want to be Columba with no Picts to convert.
I want to shuffle round the malls and bookshops in
my raincoat-canvas-habit, drawing
black but baffled looks from security staff
and making no eye contact with
the practically-famous murdering
would-be well-dressed heathen
apparently-sexy savages.
I want to be invisible.

Could everyone continue to assume
they're cleverer more talented and
better-looking than me?
Could they pay me no attention show me
no compassion find me less
than interesting? Could
they keep up the lack of passes please?
I want to stay invisible.

I wish to be a transparent parent,
an unseen companion, an undercover lover,
I wish to be a glass ship in a glass bottle.
I wish to be second banana
to Harvey the six-foot rabbit –
not even visible to Jimmy Stewart;
I wish to be second fiddle in
the Mercurian Symphony Orchestra.
I wish to be the invisible mending on
the hairline fracture between
our presence and the present;
the kind of friend who'll see through you.

I want to be the iron dove
in the magician's uncottoned-onto glove.

126

Could everyone remain in the building whilst
I dust it for God's fingerprint?
Could everyone remain in their mindsets whilst
I eliminate their continent from my enquiries?
Could everyone question themselves about the sin
I'm not forgiving them for,
you know sir, desiring a commodity
and not a society, and then
just incriminate and arrest themselves?

I'm nearly forgotten,
just one more more question.

Answermachine

Eh amna here tae tak yir caa:
Eh'm mebbe aff at thi fitbaa,
Eh mebbe amna here at aa

but jist a figment o yir filo
conjerrt up wance oan a while-o.
Therr's mebbe tatties oan thi bile-o;

Eh'm mebbe haein a wee bit greet
owre an ingin or ma sweet-
hert: or Eh'm bleedan i thi street

wi ma heid kickd in fur bein sae deep.
Eh'm mebbe here but fast asleep:
sae laive a message at thi bleep.